A Journalist's Guide to the Internet

A Journalist's Guide to the Internet

The Net as a Reporting Tool

Christopher Callahan
University of Maryland

Allyn and Bacon
Boston • London • Toronto • Sydney • Tokyo • Singapore

Vice President: Paul A. Smith
Series Editor: Karon Bowers
Editorial Production Service: Chestnut Hill Enterprises, Inc.
Manufacturing Buyer: David Repetto
Cover Administrator: Jennifer Hart

Internet: www.abacon.com

Between the time Website information is gathered and published, some sites may
have been closed. Also, the transciption of URLs can result in typographical errors.
The publisher would appreciate notification where these occur so that they may be
corrected in subsequent editions.

Library of Congress Cataloging-in-Publication Data

Callahan, Christopher.
    A journalist's guide to the Internet : the Net as a reporting tool
/ by Christopher Callahan.
      p.   cm.
    Includes index.
    ISBN 0-205-28215-6 (pbk. : alk. paper)
    1. Journalism—Data processing.   2. Internet (Computer network)
  3. Information networks.   I. Title.
  PN4784.E5c35   1999
  070.4'0285–dc21   98–39183
                                                                       CIP

Printed in the United States of America

10 9 8 7 6 5 4 3   03 02 01 00 99

To Mom and Dad

Brief Contents

Contents

▶

Preface

This is not a computer book; it is a journalism book. That is a critical distinction in understanding and using this text. There are thousands of computer books available, hundreds on the Internet alone.* This book looks at the Internet from a *journalistic* perspective: How best can reporters and editors, facing tight and unbending deadlines, use this technology accurately and effectively to improve the quality of their journalism?

The Internet—with its instant, ever-growing, and largely free access to millions of data sources around the world—provides journalists with the most important reporting tool since the telephone. But when used poorly, the Internet can be detrimental to journalism by exacerbating sloppy and inaccurate reporting. *In short, the Internet almost always will make good reporters better, and usually will make bad reporters worse.* This book attempts to provide a road map to help good reporters make their journalism better.

In Chapter 1, we look at how to think strategically about the Internet, from the perspective of reporters and editors under deadline. Chapter 2 covers the basics of navigating tools and techniques of the Net. Chapter 3 looks at how to evaluate the reliability of Internet-accessed information through a journalistic prism. The next three chapters detail some of the best Internet sites for journalists: basic resources, references, and reporters' tools are in Chapter 4, top data sites make up Chapter 5, and Chapter 6 looks at electronic news publications. In Chapter 7, we discuss targeted search strategies, and Chapter 8 describes how to build a system of Internet sites specific to news beats. Chapters 9, 10, and 11 explore other areas of the Internet—electronic mail, E-mail discussion groups, and electronic bulletin boards—and

---

*The Library of Congress listed 1,275 titles—books and periodicals—under the subject heading "Internet" by the beginning of 1998.

their potential journalistic uses. Chapter 12 shows how the Internet can be useful to journalists trying to improve their craft, keep up on new developments in the profession, or find their next jobs. The final chapter explores what the future may hold for journalists looking toward the Internet as a reporting tool. And throughout the book, some of the nation's best journalists tell their favorite stories to illustrate how the Net has worked for them.

A Journalist's Guide to the Internet is written as a practical, jargon-free guide for two audiences—college journalism students and professional reporters and editors. I hope both groups will find it useful in improving their journalism products.

—Christopher Callahan

▶

Acknowledgments

This book is possible because of the generous time and energy spent by many colleagues around the country. I would especially like to thank Sarah Cohen of Investigative Reporters and Editors, Inc., Bill Dedman, Linda Fibich of the Minneapolis *Star Tribune*, Jeff Friedson of The Prudential, Chris Harvey of washingtonpost.com, Linda Johnson of the *Lexington Herald-Leader,* Jennifer LaFleur of the *San Jose Mercury News*, Carl Sessions Stepp of the University of Maryland, and Mitchell Zuckoff of the *Boston Globe*. Each offered invaluable suggestions, guidance, and support.

I owe a special debt of gratitude to the journalists who generously contributed original essays: Jo Craven of the *Washington Post,* Steven Eisenstadt of the Raleigh *News & Observer*, Phineas Fiske of *Newsday*, Penny Loeb of *U.S. News & World Report*, Bill Loving of the Minneapolis *Star Tribune*, David Milliron of Gannett News Service, Heather Newman of the *Detroit Free Press,* Paul Overberg of *USA Today*, Neil Reisner of the *Miami Herald*, Mark Schleifstein of the New Orleans *Times-Picayune*, Ernie Slone of the *Orange County Register,* Frank Sweeney of the *San Jose Mercury News,* and Duff Wilson of the *Seattle Times.*

Kelly McInerney and Chet Rhodes of the University of Maryland were responsible for showing me the power and potential of the Internet long before it became an integral part of our culture. Chris Harvey urged me to write the book in the first place. Dean Reese Cleghorn provided me with the time and encouragement to take on this project. The reviewers—Jeffrey Brody, California State University at Fullerton; John V. Pavlik, Columbia University; and Carl Sessions Stepp, University of Maryland—provided valuable comments. Karon Bowers, my excellent editor at Allyn & Bacon, guided the book through the publishing process. And of course, my ever-patient wife, Jeanmarie, through her encouragement and support, helped me see the project through.

▶

About the Author

Christopher Callahan is assistant dean of the College of Journalism at the University of Maryland at College Park. He is a former Washington correspondent for The Associated Press. He also worked in AP bureaus in Boston, Providence, Augusta, Maine, and Concord, New Hampshire. Callahan is a graduate of Harvard University's John F. Kennedy School of Government and Boston University's School of Public Communication. He writes regularly for the *American Journalism Review (AJR)* and is a member of AJR's Board of Editorial Advisers. He specializes in political and governmental reporting, investigative reporting, diversity issues in the newsroom, and uses of the Internet for journalists.

A Journalist's Guide to the Internet is an outgrowth of Callahan's research into practical uses of the Internet for reporters and editors on deadline. He has delivered seminars and workshops on the Internet for a wide variety of professional journalists and journalism organizations, including Investigative Reporters and Editors, the Society of Professional Journalists, *USA Today*, The Associated Press, the National Institute for Computer-Assisted Reporting, Voice of America, the National Conference of Editorial Writers, the Maryland–Delaware District Press Association, the Hubert H. Humphrey International Journalism Fellows, and the Alfred Friendly Press Fellows.

Callahan has been in journalism education since 1989, teaching graduate and undergraduate courses at the University of Maryland at College Park, Columbia College of Chicago, and Boston University. He also is director of Capital News Service, the University of Maryland's advanced public affairs reporting program in Washington and Annapolis, executive director of the Maryland Scholastic Press Association for high school journalism students and advisers, and faculty adviser to the University of Maryland chapter of the Society of Professional Journalists.

He lives in Great Falls, Virginia, with his wife, Jeanmarie, and their two children, Cody and Casey. His personal Web site is at reporter.umd.edu/

▶ 1

Journalists and the Net

I don't like computers. Never did really. I suspect I was the victim of bad timing. I was a journalism student in Boston in the late 1970s, just as computers were sweeping into newsrooms across the nation, but before they became commonplace in journalism classrooms. In my first job as a reporter in the wilds of northern New England, the computers crashed so often that they made me long for the days of banging out stories on the battered gray Royals back at the campus daily. But despite the early frustrations, writing on the computer—with the ability to quickly change words and sentences and move around chunks of a story—made our jobs easier, and our journalism products better.

Not long after my fledgling forays into the computer world, commercial databases began springing up, giving reporters the ability to quickly access background for stories on deadline. Systems such as Nexis–Lexis, though expensive, became important additions to the journalist's reporting arsenal, and the systems were fairly easy to use. They came with directories of files and standardized keyword search systems. Many reporters today could not imagine trying to background a story without an electronic database.

Today, the new frontier for computer-savvy journalists is the Internet.

WHAT IS THE INTERNET?

The Internet has seemingly come from nowhere to be omnipresent in our culture in the past few years. In fact, the Internet is more than 20 years old, a creation of the Defense Department. Unlike commercial databases such as Nexis–Lexis, there is no Internet Corp., no single institution called the Internet. Instead, the Internet is, at its essence, simply a network of attached

1

computer networks. The Internet system allows users to go from one computer network to another. Users can quickly move from a college in New England to a library in Australia to a military installation in California. Users can be said to be "on" the Internet, but they are "in" the Australian library, New England college, or California military base. This is a critically important distinction for journalists trying to evaluate the accuracy and value of the information they are finding.

Although it has been around for decades, the Internet was used mostly by the military and academia until recent years. Technological advancements in the early 1990s led to the creation of the World Wide Web, a graphically oriented part of the Internet that allows users to point and click on text, images, audio, and video. The intuitive point-and-shoot design of the Web was much easier to master than the earlier architectures of the Internet and led to extraordinary growth. It is impossible to estimate how many people are on the Internet. Instead, analysts look at the growth in computer systems connected to the Internet. By most estimates, that has been roughly *doubling* each year. Network Wizards (www.nw.com), a Silicon Valley computer firm that conducts a biannual survey, estimates that the number of computer systems connected to the Internet has mushroomed from less than 1.8 million in July 1993 to nearly 30 million by January 1997—a 16-fold increase in just four years.

The Network Wizards graphic (see Figure 1.1) shows the staggering growth in computer systems connected to the Internet during the 1990s.

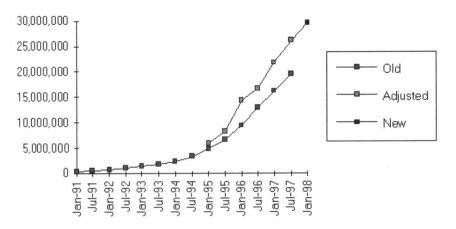

FIGURE 1.1   Internet Domain Survey Host Count

Source: Network Wizards, www.nw.com

WHY SHOULD JOURNALISTS CARE ABOUT THE INTERNET?

Today the Internet stands as the single largest source of information available anywhere in the world. And from a reporter's perspective, the Net will only get better as more and more information is added. The possibilities for information-hungry journalists are limitless. It also is relatively inexpensive, as low as $10 or so a month for unlimited use. That stands in stark contrast to many of the bill-by-the-minute commercial databases that can run a newsroom tens of thousands of dollars a year. But there's a catch. Because of the way the Internet has grown up—in a piecemeal fashion without much design or forethought—there is no one single way to search comprehensively for information. That can leave the unprepared journalist frustrated, with nothing to show for his or her efforts other than hours wasted surfing around the Net, busted deadlines, and angry editors. And the incredible growth of the Web can add to a reporter's frustration, with sites coming and going daily and addresses constantly changing.

In the final analysis, is it worth the hassle? Yes, without question. Reporters around the country have developed stories that they would never have been able to do—or stories that would have been too costly or too time-intensive to go after—without the Internet. Throughout this book, we will hear from journalists who have used the Internet to track tornadoes in Minnesota, investigate the state of fisheries and wetlands, analyze standardized tests in elementary schools, and detail how recycled hazardous waste gets into fertilizer. And that's not to mention the less sexy but just as important everyday uses that help save valuable time and add depth to breaking news stories.

Does that mean that if you are not an Internet expert you will never be a great journalist? Of course not. Many of the best journalists in the country don't know a Web site from a spider web, but continue to produce award-winning journalism. It does mean, however, that having the basic skills of Internet reporting will make your journalism better—in some cases through saved time that can be put into other aspects of a story, sometimes through more in-depth reporting, and in other cases through new stories not available elsewhere.

THINKING STRATEGICALLY ABOUT THE NET

In talking with journalists around the country, I find a large number who have given the Net a whirl, only to get frustrated with its idiosyncrasies and give up on it all together. The problem is not the Net, but lack of a strategic plan to attack it. Many journalists and journalism students approach the Internet as they would a commercial database. That is to say, facing a deadline,

BOX 1.1

Duff Wilson, an investigative reporter at the Seattle Times, *explains how he used the Internet to help show how toxic wastes were getting into farm fertilizer.*

At least 10 states and the federal government are scrutinizing toxic wastes in fertilizer because of *Seattle Times* reports that would have been simply impossible without the Internet.

The Web was my worldwide medical librarian, agronomist, biologist, toxicologist, lawyer, regulator, and, of course, telephone operator and postal carrier. So it seemed. I used Web sites, newsgroups, and E-mail almost every day during and after publication.

"Fear in the Fields—How hazardous wastes become fertilizer" was an in-depth series of articles published starting July 3, 1997. (www.seattletimes.com/news/special/index.html#fields)

The articles showed how some heavy industries save millions of dollars by disposing of hazardous wastes as fertilizer and other farm soil supplements.

All over the United States, farmers were unknowingly using this recycled waste—sometimes with calamitous results they couldn't understand. And this was all being done legally, in the name of recycling, with virtually no governmental oversight or regulation.

I learned about this problem from the whistle-blowing mayor of the small farm town of Quincy, Washington. Her opponents—the big farms and chemical companies—tried to shut her up by threatening to sue her for another Alar "scare." The Web helped me document the complaints carefully,

though, and put Quincy in a national and global context.

Among the Internet tools that were most helpful:

- Industrial Material Exchange sites, quiet little corners of the Web where waste brokers sell or give away toxic materials. I compared them to blind-dating services.
- Medline, the free index to 9 million medical journal articles from around the world. Many of the non-English ones have English language summaries. This service from the National Library of Medicine gets my vote for the most helpful site on the Web. One of my best searches cross-matched *cadmium* and *fertilizer.*
- Experts of every stripe dug up from DejaNews, Liszt, and Reference.com newsgroups and mailing lists.
- The Right-to-Know Network's database covering the Environmental Protection Agency's Toxic Release Inventory. I found official government reports on industries sending hazardous wastes to fertilizer manufacturers.

In addition, I used general search engines to find a wealth of information about heavy metals and dioxins and fertilizer. Yahoo is my favorite search engine because of its generosity in linking to other search engines.

BOX 1.1 *Continued*

Yahoo eventually led me to a Colorado company, CoZinCo, that was publishing chemical analyses of fertilizer products. They showed up to 5 percent lead contents, and, as I found out through other Web articles as well as interviews and tree-killing material (paperwork), the lead can be very dangerous indeed.

Since the articles were published, people from around the world have tuned in through our *Seattle Times* Web site. I also used the Internet to send out every article as it was published in this corner of the country to an informal mailing list of more than 50 people around the globe. This way, they could read the full versions, and I could immediately solicit their follow-up ideas and their all-important input on the fairness, accuracy, and completeness of each article.

they jump on the Net, punch in a few key words and begin "surfing" around. After a few tries—and failures—they get off-line as quickly as they jumped on. Let me recommend a more targeted, tiered approach that will cut down on frustration while improving results and boosting confidence.

Reliable Sites. Forget "surfing," at least at the beginning. The first foray into using the Internet in a deadline reporting setting should be simply to begin using sites that you know are going to lead to the sought-after information. Chapters 4, 5, and 6 detail more than 100 of the best Internet sites available for journalists today. Focusing on this method will build your confidence in both the Internet's ability to help your reporting and in your ability to use the Internet.

Think Past the Rolodex. The Internet provides reporters with the opportunity to get beyond their Rolodex list of usual sources, providing greater depth and breadth to their journalism. It is especially useful for tapping into state and federal government sources for information affecting the local community. Traditionally, community-based reporters have paid little attention to state and federal matters because of geographic constraints. But now, for instance, a reporter covering a single town can use the Internet to access detailed financial records on the area's biggest employers from the Securities and Exchange Commission, find out who locally is contributing to the upcoming congressional campaigns from a federal contributions database, and get a jump on the Pentagon's plans for the local military installation from the Federal Register. We will look at this in more depth in Chapter 8.

Build an Electronic Beat System. In the next chapter we will discuss how reporters can save and organize the Internet sites they have discovered.

This idea can be expanded into creating a personalized series of files that hold computer sites that you may use on your beat. Chapter 8 is devoted to conceptualizing an electronic beat system and how to create one for yourself.

BOX 1.2

The Internet played a critical role in a bankruptcy project headed by David Milliron, special projects editor at Gannett News Service.

Despite a booming economy and the lowest unemployment rates in a generation, a record 1 million Americans headed into bankruptcy court in 1996 to fold their financial cards and ask for a new game. Gannett News Service wanted to know how the bankruptcy rate had grown, and where, down to the local level. The Internet was key to locating the necessary data for the project, which was published in March 1997. GNS revisited the issue of bankruptcies in February 1998.

The Internet led GNS to the American Bankruptcy Institute (ABI) in Alexandria, Virginia. The ABI publishes a multitude of bankruptcy statistics and analyses. A phone call to the ABI's data specialist pointed us to a data contact at the Administrative Office of the U.S. Courts, which told us the agency had a county-by-county database of aggregate bankruptcy data.

- Both personal and business filings, by type of filing, dating back to fiscal year 1991.
- The data, exclusively obtained for the first time by GNS, are kept in a popular word processing file format.

While awaiting delivery of the data, GNS continued gathering background for the package. Here are some of the useful Internet sites GNS used:

- The American Bankruptcy Institute site (at www.abiworld.org) contains a news section with bankruptcy news headlines from newspapers, press releases, and other sources, plus a bankruptcy library section, and a section on legislative news.
- The U.S. Courts' Home Page (at www.uscourts.gov) provided information on the various types of bankruptcy filings, the number of bankruptcy judges, and contacts at the Administrative Office of the U.S. Courts.
- Federal Filings Online (at www. fedfil.com/index.htm) provided the latest bankruptcy news, the status of major bankruptcy cases, and a list of other bankruptcy-related Internet links.
- The Federal Reserve site (at www. bog.frb.fed.us) contains "Domestic and International Research Statistics," which has links to current and historical data, including the monthly "G.19" consumer credit report.
- The National Bankruptcy Review Commission site (at www.nbrc. gov) provided background documents and testimony being gathered for its presidential report on the state of the bankruptcy system.

BOX 1.3

Jo Craven, a member of the Washington Post *computer-assisted reporting team, used the Internet in a variety of ways for a major investigation into the Unification Church.*

Time was short: *Washington Post* reporters Marc Fisher and Jeff Leen were given less than a month to explore the operation of the Reverend Sun Myung Moon, a religious leader with a reputation for using a variety of businesses to gently weave his way into the fabric of a community. His motivation, church leaders and critics said, is to provide employment to his followers, to gain influence in industries he considers crucial for recognition of himself as Messiah, and to support his spiritual and political agenda.

Because Moon's operation—dubbed Moon Inc. by Fisher and Leen—spans continents, the reporters decided to concentrate on the Washington metro area, and the Internet provided a helpful jump-start to the project.

Researcher Alice Crites combed the Net for information on Moon and came up with a list of possible connections—businesses, including seafood companies, media groups, jewelers, dance troupes, and others with an estimated value of $300 million—that we suspected were owned or sponsored by Moon and his circle.

The next step was to prove the connection.

Using a dial-up bulletin board system (BBS) operated by the Virginia Corporation Commission, I checked the incorporation papers of more than 30 businesses and found the links we were looking for; while Moon and his known allies were rarely listed as owner or president of the companies, time and again, I found one or more of them listed in the next tier, as officers or directors.

As we unraveled Moon's connections to these companies, Fisher and Leen called on many of them, and, in a very short time, stitched together a comprehensive profile of Moon Inc.

We also used a variety of other Internet resources, with varying success: On the off-chance that some of the companies might be publicly held, Crites and I checked Securities and Exchange Commission records on the Internet; I used several on-line phone and E-mail directories to help Fisher locate some sources outside of the Washington area; and I used another BBS to search for lawsuits against Moon.

While all of the records we searched are available, often with more detail, on paper, accessing them electronically gave us what we needed and saved us a lot of time on a tight deadline.

Think Institutionally. Once the top Web sites from Chapters 4, 5, and 6 have been incorporated into your reporter's toolbox, you will be ready to search for specific information. In commercial database searches, we use keyword searches. If we are researching a story on the growth of women farmers and want statistics, we might type in keywords such as *women* and *farmers* into a commercial database. But such a search likely would produce poor results on the Internet because of its vastness. A better approach would be to think institutionally. What institution—association, organization, governmental agency, lobbying group, company—might have the information we are seeking? Instead of using *women* and *farmers* as the Internet keywords, we might instead look for "likely suspects," institutions that are likely to have the information. In this case, the Census Bureau and the U.S. Department of Agriculture might be logical places to search. Thinking institutionally in Internet searches can save valuable time. We will explore this strategy more in Chapter 7.

Search Engines as the Last Resort. Searching by institution only works if you have some idea what institutions may have the information you are seeking. If you don't know, then you must plunge into the final frontier of the Internet for journalists: surfing for information with directories and search engines. This is the most used method by nonjournalists, but for deadline-conscious reporters, it should be the least frequently employed method. We will explore various searching strategies and specific search engines in Chapter 7.

Before we begin our journey into the world of journalistic uses of the Internet, we need to know a little bit about how to get around the Net and evaluate the information we find there.

▶ 2

Navigating the Net

GETTING STARTED ON-LINE

Hopefully your newsroom or classroom already is wired to the Internet. If not, you may have to convince your editor or professor to get your institution hooked up, or you may have to get connected on your own. The first decision is whether to get a direct Internet connection through a local Internet provider, or to subscribe to one of the big services such as CompuServe or America Online (AOL). The advantage of CompuServe and AOL is that, in addition to an Internet connection, they provide customers with their own content. While that content is minuscule compared to the information available on the Internet, it can be helpful to reporters because—unlike the Net—it is well-organized and has things such as archived newspapers and magazines that are not readily available on the Net. They are, of course, more expensive than the direct Internet connections. If you already have easy access to electronic newspaper archives through other sources in your newsroom or classroom, then save the extra money and go with a direct Internet connection. If you cannot access newspaper archives, you may want to look at CompuServe or AOL. And, whenever possible, get a subscription that charges a flat fee for unlimited access. Unlimited use Internet connections are as low as $10 a month under longer term contracts.

Once a provider has been selected, the only other thing you need, assuming you already have access to a Windows-based computer, is a modem. The rule of thumb is simple: Get the fastest one available. A slow modem can make working on the Internet under deadline a painful experience. If you are just now buying a modem, you can probably get one that has more capacity than your Internet service can provide. That's okay. Things in cyberspace develop quickly, and your Internet provider will eventually catch up to your new modem.

THE WORLD WIDE WEB

Just a few short years ago, Internet users had to navigate in a fairly complex computer environment. Today, the Internet is dominated by the World Wide Web, a graphically oriented, user-friendly portion of the Internet that has seen enormous growth in recent years. With few exceptions, the Web is where the action is for journalists and nonjournalists alike, and it will be the main focus of this book.

The basic workings of the Web are relatively simple (from the users' vantage point). Users browse through a Web page filled with text and graphical images. Some of the text and graphics may be highlighted. Users point and click on the highlighted portion of the page and are sent to another Web page, either in that same computer system or into an entirely different system.

NETSCAPE NAVIGATOR VS. MICROSOFT EXPLORER

Two software "browser" programs designed to navigate the Web dominate usage today: Netscape's Navigator (Figure 2.1) and Microsoft's Internet Explorer (Figure 2.2). They are similar in design, but, like everything in the computer world, they trigger great debate. Some people believe Netscape is by far the superior product, while others insist Explorer is the way to go. The truth is, people usually like best whichever they started out with. I use Netscape's Navigator not because it is better than Microsoft's Explorer, but because that is what I learned on. If you have a relatively new computer, it is probably loaded with both already. If not, both will be available through your Internet provider. And you can download new versions of the software for free.

SOFTWARE OVERVIEW

Let's take a moment to go over some of the basic features of the navigation software that reporters would likely need. Most of the illustrations will be from Netscape Navigator, but I will include descriptions of Internet Explorer when the functions are different from Netscape. Also note that each company releases updated versions of the software regularly.

Once connected to the Internet, click on the software icon. A preprogrammed "home page" will pop onto the screen. A home page is the main page of a Web computer site. Your new software will be programmed for

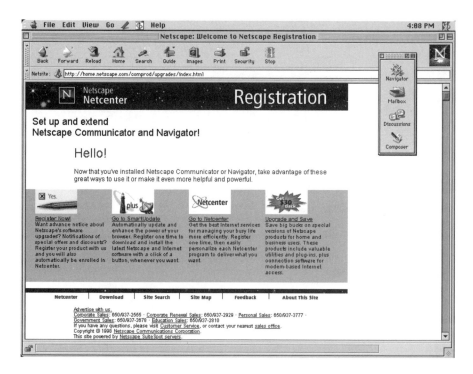

FIGURE 2.1   Netscape Navigator

either the software manufacturer's home page or the computer manufacturer's home page, either of which is useless for reporters. We will discuss
how to change the home page in a bit. But first, some basics.

Near the top of the program is a white box (called "Location" in
Netscape Navigator and "Address" in Internet Explorer). That gives you the
computer address of the Web site that is currently on the screen. It is vital to
keep a close eye on this box in order to determine where you are at all times
in order to evaluate the reliability of the information.

The power of the Web is in "hyperlinks." Hyperlinks, or simply "links,"
will take a user to another section of the same Web page, to another page on
the same computer site, or to a completely different site, all with a simple
mouse click. You can see what has links by passing your mouse arrow over
the text and graphics. If there is a link, the arrow will turn into a hand with
an extended index finger pointing at the linked object. Linked text also
stands out in a different color from the nonlinked portion of the text, usually
in blue. To go to the link site, single click with your mouse.

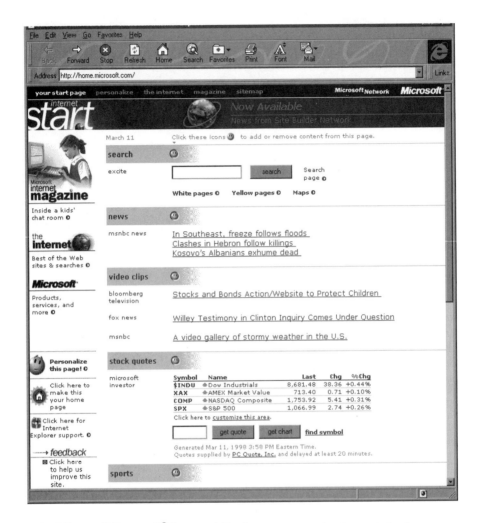

FIGURE 2.2   Microsoft® Internet Explorer. Reprinted with permission from Microsoft Corporation.

This point-and-click method is both the beauty and the problem with the Web. It is easy to get from one place to another, but too often users will go clicking through a site and soon do not know where they are or how they got there. That is why it is critical to keep your eye on the Web address. Even before clicking on a link, you can see the new address by placing the mouse pointer over the linked material. The linked address will appear in the bottom left portion of your screen. The following are some basic Web navigation tools and techniques.

Stop Right There!

It is important to be aware of what the computer is doing at any given time. Depending on the speed of your connection and the complexity of the graphics on the page being accessed, it could take some time before the page is fully loaded. To observe whether the screen is still downloading, look at the corporate icon in the top right corner of the screen. If it is moving, that means the last command is still being performed. The command is completed when the icon stops moving. The results of the command also can be viewed in the lower left-hand corner, which shows the computer opening up the file. When it is completed, Netscape tells you "Document: Done." For graphic-laden Web sites on slow-moving modems, you may decide you simply want to cancel your last command. To do that, go up to the command bar and click on the red stop sign in Netscape or the red X in Explorer.

Getting Rid of Graphics

Graphics make Web pages eye-catching, but they do little for journalists other than slow down our reporting, especially for those who do not have high-speed connections to the Internet. You may want to consider turning off the graphics. That leaves you with just text, but greatly speeds up the downloading process. To turn off the graphics in Netscape, go the Options menu and click on Auto Load Images. That will remove the check mark. To turn the graphics back on, repeat the command and the check mark will reappear. In Explorer, go to the View menu and select Options. Click on Appearance and remove the checks from the top three boxes—Show Pictures, Play Sounds, and Show Animations—to remove the check marks.

Moving Backward and Forward

Among the most important software tools are the Back and Forward commands. You can "surf" around a site—the process of clicking from one page to another via hyperlinks—and then if you decide what was really needed was something two clicks ago, simply "back out" by using the Back button (a left arrow in Explorer). Each click on the Back button will take you to the previous page. The Forward button (a right arrow in Explorer) will take you ahead to points where you had been previously before backing out. Netscape and Explorer also leave a "footprint" on links that have been used recently by changing the traditionally blue linked text to a different color, enabling you to retrace your steps.

Bookmarks

Each program also enables users to save the addresses of useful Web sites. When you come across a site you may want to return to, pull down the Bookmarks menu and go to Add Bookmark. The next time you want to go to that site, go back to the Bookmarks menu and pull down to the saved site. The Go To Bookmarks function under the Bookmarks menu allows users to organize their saved Web sites in folders. We will be working with this function extensively in the chapter on creating an electronic beat system. (In Explorer, Bookmarks are called "Favorites." Explorer users go to the folder icon with a + sign to Add To Favorites and to the adjoining folder icon to Go To Favorites.)

Print, Find, and Save

Both programs have print buttons that will print out the full Web page you have open on the screen. If a file is too long you may want to save it onto your computer hard drive or floppy disk and read it later. To save a file into a word processing program, go to the File menu and select Save As (same in both programs). There will be other times when you are looking for a very small piece of information in a very large document. Instead of downloading the entire document into your word processor, you can click on the Find icon in Netscape and type in a keyword or phrase. Find will take you directly to the word or words you are seeking.

Go Directly to a Site

The next section of this book, Chapters 4, 5, and 6, details specific Web sites. To get to those sites, or any other sites for which you know the specific address, simply go to the Location box in Netscape (or the Address box in Explorer) and type in the address. Note that, as you begin making the change, the Location box name turns to "Go to:" (and Explorer's Address box turns to "Open"). Alternatively, you can click on the Open icon in Netscape (Open File icon on the top right side in Explorer) and type in the address. Either way, be sure the address is precise. A misplaced comma, an extra letter or a dot instead of a slash will result in a failed search. Also note that in newer versions of Navigator and Explorer, the programs automatically add the http:// to the beginning of all addresses.

Searching

Search engines are used when you do not have a specific Web address. We will discuss search engines and search strategies at length in Chapter 7, but for now it is enough to know that there are many search engines out there, they all work differently, and there is no single search engine that can comprehensively search all of the Internet. To easily access some of the major search engines, click on the Net Search button on Netscape under the Location box. On this page Netscape has linked to a handful of the most popular and powerful search engines, including Yahoo, Infoseek, Lycos, and WebCrawler. Much like the personal preferences for Navigator or Explorer, everyone who has ever been on the Net has a favorite search engine and swears by it. The reality, however, is that we should use different search engines for different situations. But, again, we will explore search engines and strategies in Chapter 7.

Changing the Home Page

As we discussed earlier, the browser software comes with a preprogrammed home page that appears every time you go on-line. It usually advertises the software you are using or the computer you have just bought or something equally useless for a deadline reporter. Instead, the home page can be changed to a site that a reporter might actually want to look at and use in daily reporting. Some options include your own newspaper, your local news competition, a dominant regional newspaper (such as the *Boston Globe* for New England reporters), or a national publication (such as the *New York Times* or *Washington Post*). The home page also could be the Web site of an institution you cover regularly, such as the U.S. Congress Web site for a congressional correspondent or the state higher education board for a campus reporter. Or you can make the page a journalism reference, such as Investigative Reporters and Editors or the *American Journalism Review.* The best option may be to make the home page one of the many reporter's toolboxes that are available on the Internet. These are Web sites created by journalists to assist you in using the Internet in your reporting. Many of the sites listed in Chapters 4, 5, 6, and 12 are available at the author's Web-based reporter's toolbox at:

reporter.umd.edu

To change the home page on Navigator, go to the Options menu and pull down to Preferences. Click on Appearances and, inside the Startup box, type in the address of the Web site you want to be your opening page. In Internet Explorer, call up the page you want to be your home page, then go to the View menu and pull down Options. Click on the Start and Search Pages, click on the Use Current button and then the OK button. The home button icon on Navigator (and house icon on Explorer) will bring you back to your home page.

Now that we know the basics of navigating the Web, let's look at how to evaluate the information we find.

Evaluating Information from the Internet

MYTHS ABOUT THE INTERNET AND CREDIBILITY

There are a lot of misconceptions about the Internet, particularly when talking about the reliability of information found there. Some people—and I am afraid students fall into this category more than most—seem to place a credibility blanket over the Net. If it is on the Net, the thinking goes, it must be right.

Then there is the other extreme, folks—and some veteran editors and reporters seem to be in this camp—who have heard about the rumor-mongering and other bad information floating around in cyberspace and immediately dismiss everything on the Net as not credible.

The problem with both ways of thinking is that they conceptualize the Internet as a single entity. As we discussed in Chapter 1, the Internet is not an information source in itself; it is, rather, a conduit to get to various sources of information. Therefore, it does not matter whether the information was obtained via the Internet. What matters is where that information came from, the original source. Dismissing or accepting information simply because it was obtained from the Internet is the equivalent of rejecting or embracing information simply because it came from a newspaper, book, or magazine. In traditional reporting, we do not evaluate information based on its form; we evaluate it on the credibility of the source that is producing the information. Both the *New York Times* and the *National Enquirer* are newspapers, printed products that disseminate news in paper form. But we place different levels of credibility on information in those publications based on our knowledge of the products. That is the same analysis we must perform when evaluating information on the Internet.

WHAT'S OUT THERE?

While the analysis we perform to determine credibility is the same, whether the information comes in printed paper form or digitally, the Internet does make the job a bit more cumbersome for one reason: It is much cheaper to "publish" on the Internet than to publish a book, newspaper, magazine, or report. Therefore, there is a lot more junk on the Net. In fact, the overwhelming majority of what can be found on the Internet could never be used in a news story. Then why bother? Simple. The Internet is so vast, even if only a small fraction of the information available meets our journalistic litmus tests for credibility, that still represents an enormous amount of valuable information that otherwise might be difficult or expensive or time-consuming to obtain.

DECODING WEB ADDRESSES

To evaluate the credibility of Internet-gathered information, a reporter must determine the source of that information. And the key to determining the source of information is to decode the World Wide Web address. A basic Web address consists of a series of letters, which often form words, separated by periods, which in Internet parlance are referred to as *dots.* For instance, the main address for the White House is:

www.whitehouse.gov

Let's deconstruct this address. The "www" stands for the World Wide Web. Most (but not all) Web sites begin with www. Next "whitehouse" is clearly descriptive of the Web site. Finally, we see the suffix "gov." That stands for government. Web addresses end in a similar three-letter code that indicates, generally, what type of entity is publishing the Web site. When analyzing Web sites, immediately go to the suffix. Some common suffixes in the United States include:

.gov = Government bodies, including federal, state, and local government departments, agencies, and officials

.edu = Education, including colleges and universities

.mil = U.S. military sites

.org = Nonprofit organizations and associations

.int = International organizations

.com = Commercial

.net = Networking organizations

Government and Military Sites

Analyzing the suffixes goes a long way in helping to determine the source. Only official government entities are allowed to use the .gov suffix. Does that mean everything found on the Internet with the .gov suffix is reliable and credible? Of course not, just as every government official or every government document is not reliable and credible. What can be concluded is that information found on the Internet with a .gov address has come from the White House, or state Education Department, or City Council. And once the source has been determined, the Internet-accessed information from those entities can be treated in the same way as information received in paper form. The same is true of the .mil suffix. The .mil suffix shows that the Web site is run by a branch of the Defense Department and should be evaluated accordingly.

Educational Institutions

The .edu site is not quite as clear-cut. Only educational institutions—colleges and universities—are given Web addresses with the .edu suffix. But those institutions often give their students the ability to publish on the Web. That's great for free speech and expression, but not so great for journalists who need to know whether the information is coming from Harvard University or the 18-year-old freshman sitting in his dorm room at 3 A.M. and sharing the meaning of life with the world. Needless to say, it is usually self-evident which site is from the student and which is from a bunch of academics and administrators (for one, the student site is almost always more creative). But reporters, who should have a healthy dose of skepticism about getting the cyber-wool pulled over their eyes, should make sure that what looks like the Harvard Law School site is not really a *Lampoon* spoof. Here is a simple way: College sites have addresses that refer to their subdivisions. For instance, the Web address for the University of Maryland's College of Journalism is:

www.inform.umd.edu/jour

Here, we see the main address for the university: "www" for the World Wide Web, "inform" is the name of the system at Maryland, "umd" stands for the University of Maryland, "edu" is the suffix ensuring us that the Web site is from a bona fide institution of higher learning, and "jour" is the university's abbreviation for Journalism. Student sites usually have their name or some nickname in their address. Student John Smith's Maryland address, for instance, might look like this:

www.wam.umd.edu/~jsmith/home.htm

Another way to ensure the credibility of a university-based Internet site is to get on the institution's main page and point and click to the site that contains the information being evaluated. Colleges traditionally link only to their own Web pages, not to students' individual sites.

Nonprofit Organizations

Nonprofit organizations and associations pose a different problem for reporters. A Web address with the .org suffix ensures that the information is coming from a nonprofit organization, in much the same way the .gov suffix guarantees that the site is from a governmental body. And the same rules should apply. Say you received information from www.nra.org. This is the Internet site for the National Rifle Association. Should you conclude that all of the information you find on www.nra.org is 100 percent right (or 100 percent wrong)? No. You should determine simply that the information came from the NRA, and weigh that information in the same fashion that you would analyze it if you received it in a more traditional form. The problem is, governmental agencies have a certain level of credibility and recognition. Reporters may, however, come across nonprofit organizations on the Internet that are unknown to them. The response in these cases should be the same as if the reporters were sent a press release or report from a group they never heard of: Check it out to determine the organization's credibility and whether they have particular biases. Who operates the group? Who is on its board? How long has it been in existence? Has it been used as an expert source of information by other press outlets?

International Sites

International organizations, such as the United Nations and NATO, carry the .int suffix. Individual country Web sites carry a two-initial suffix, an abbreviation of that country's name. For example, .au is Australia, .jp is Japan, and .ru is Russia.

Commercial Sites

The .com suffix denotes a commercial Web site. In other words, the .com Web site found can be from absolutely anybody in the world who has paid the relatively small fee to get a registered Web address. Everyone from IBM to the kid down the block can have a .com address. Needless to say, this is the most problematic area for reporters on the Internet. It would be easy—and safe—to simply ignore all .com sites, but that would eliminate some of the richest reportorial sites on the Net. Instead, treat the .com sites the same as an .org address. If you know the company, say IBM, then evaluate the information as you would the same information in paper form from the company. If it is a commercial entity you never heard of, make sure you check it out.

The two Web sites shown in Figures 3.1 and 3.2 have similar looks and similar addresses. Only the last part of the Web address is different. Figure 3.1, located at www.whitehouse.gov, is the official Internet site of the president of the United States. Figure 3.2, located at www.whitehouse.net, is Why InterNetworking, a Web development company. There is also a site at www.whitehouse.com, a pornography site that clearly has nothing to do with the White House. Remember, always check the suffix first when trying to determine where you are.

TECHNIQUES FOR EVALUATING WEB SITE CREDIBILITY

Finding Web Page Owners and Operators

The InterNIC, a cooperative of the National Science Foundation, Network Solutions, Inc., and AT&T, distributes and keeps tracks of all Web addresses. An InterNIC database allows users to find out the names, phone numbers, and E-mail addresses of the operators of every Web site. Reporters can type in either a "domain name"—the main part of an Internet address—to find out who operates the site, or input individuals' names to find out about any Web sites they may operate. The address is:

rs.internic.net/cgi-bin/whois

Truncating Web Addresses

Search engines (see Chapter 7) often will present matches that are deep inside a Web site. For instance, my biographical information at the University of Maryland is located at:

www.inform.umd.edu/JOUR/FacultyStaff/callahan/callahan.html

By going directly to that address, it might not be clear what organization is sponsoring the site. To find out, simply cut off all of the information to the right of the first forward slash. That leaves just the main home page, which will indicate the sponsoring institution.

This method also is useful when a Web address produced by a search engine is no longer functioning. Web sites change often, and it could be that the information is still inside that Web site, but on a different page. To find out, truncate the address and search on the main page for the item being sought.

Good Afternoon

Welcome to the
White House

The President & Vice President:
Their accomplishments, their families,
and how to send them electronic mail --

Interactive Citizens' Handbook:
Your guide to information about
the Federal government

White House History and Tours:
Past Presidents and First Families, Art
in the President's House and Tours --
Tour Information

The Virtual Library:
Search White House documents, listen
to speeches, and view photos

White House Help Desk:
Frequently asked questions and answers
about our service

**Commonly Requested Federal
Services:**
Direct access to Federal Services

What's New:
What's happening at the White
House -
**- President Clinton Calls For Steps To
Improve Health Care For American
Families**

Site News:
Recent additions to our site -
-President's Initiative on Race
-White House Millennium Council

The Briefing Room:
Today's releases, hot topics, and the
latest Federal statistics

White House for Kids:
Helping young people become more
active and informed citizens

To comment on this service, send feedback to the <u>Web Development Team</u> *.*

FIGURE 3.1

[Text version]

Welcome to the White House

The President & Vice President:
Their accomplishments, their families, and how to send them electronic mail.

Interactive Citizens' Handbook:
Your guide to information and services from the Federal government.

The LAW:
Join the Ladies Against Women as they fight for Servile Liberties and the right of Ladies everywhere.

Why?:
Because we like you.

What's New:
The President signs the Ethics in Biotechnology Act of 1998, promoting the highest moral standards in developing new medical technologies.

Help the BMS:
The Bureau of Missing Socks is the first organization solely devoted to solving the question of what happens to missing single socks.

The Briefing Room:
The President prefers these to boxers.

Executive Fan Mail:
Comments from you, the American people.

To comment on this service, send feedback to the Web Development Team.

FIGURE 3.2

Beware of Title Pages

A final warning involves the titles of Web pages. Look above the Location box and menu bar to the top of the browser software window and you will see a title. It can be helpful while reporting, but remember, it is simply a description written by the author of that page. My personal home page is titled (cleverly) "Christopher Callahan," but I could have just as easily titled it "White House" or "The Boston Red Sox" or "King George," so be wary about page titles.

TRAVELING IN AND OUT OF WEB SITES

The hyperlinks that we talked about in Chapter 2 can take you to one of three places on the Internet: to another place on the Web page you already have opened, to another page within the Web site, or to an entirely different Web site. For reporters, it is critical to always know where you are. Most Web sites have links to other sites, and if you are not paying close attention to the location box on top, you may think you are in the Web site you started in when in fact you are in an entirely different institution. This is not terribly important to the casual Internet surfer, but critical for reporters who need to evaluate the credibility of the information they are collecting. And just because one institution has links to an outside site does not mean that entity is giving its endorsement to the information in the linked site. For instance, the *Washington Post* provides its electronic readers with hyperlinks to area schools. That does not mean that the information in the schools' Web site should be evaluated in the same way as the original content of the *Washington Post*.

Even traveling within the same site can be confusing. Think of a single Web site as an underground building. You first enter the ground floor on the home page and then travel deeper into the building. Each "floor" is separated by a forward slash. So when you click one flight down, the address in the Location box will look something like this:

www.university.edu/departments.

Go down one more flight and it might look like this:

www.university.edu/departments/journalism

And still another flight down:

www.university.edu/departments/journalism/courses

The number of "floors" is limitless; therefore, in large Web sites, the addresses can get pretty complicated. Also, each "floor" can have separate pages, so the underground building begins to look more like an underground pyramid.

NEWSROOM POLICIES
FOR INTERNET REPORTING

There are few written newsroom policies or guidelines about evaluating and attributing information found on the Internet, and the policies that do exist are often general. The Associated Press Guidelines for Responsible Use of Electronic Services is typical: "Apply the strictest standards of accuracy to anything you find on electronic services. The Internet is not an authority; authorities may use it, but so do quacks.... E-mail addresses and Web page sponsorship can easily be faked. Ask yourself, 'Could this be a hoax?' Do not publish...any electronic address without testing to see that it's a working address and satisfying yourself that it is genuine. Apply, in other words, your usual news judgment."

In fact, the "usual news judgment" recommended by the AP should be the mantra of journalists reporting out on the Internet. The form of the information received does not matter; what matters is the news value of the information and the legitimacy of the person or organization putting it out. If a group unknown in your newsroom comes out with a report, it does not matter whether that report was obtained via the fax, phone, mail, news conference, or Web site. The same process used to check out the organization should be employed.

And the information, if it is to be used in a news report, should be attributed in the same way. There should not be separate, new rules of attribution for information found on the Internet. If it is important to the story to mention how the news was obtained, and sometimes it is, then that should be included. But otherwise, routinely adding that the information was found on a company's Web site is the same as reporting that the information was transmitted to the reporter via a facsimile machine.

Now that we know a bit about how to get around the Web and how to critically evaluate what we have found, it is time to see what is out there for journalists.

▶ 4

Basic Reporting Resources and References

People seem to be having an awful lot of fun on the Internet. Even those who are not on-line can read print stories about people spending countless hours listening to their favorite bands, learning about quirky hobbies or special interests that delight the mind and warm the heart, shopping 'til their fingers drop, connecting with old friends via E-mail, and finding new ones in warm and fuzzy chat rooms where people sign off with smiley faces :).

This chapter is about none of the above. What we are going to explore is how serious journalists and journalism students can employ the Internet to better use some of the most basic reporting resources and reference tools for reporters and editors. In all of these cases, using these tools via the Internet is either cheaper, faster, easier, or a combination of all three.

BOX 4.1

This chapter, along with Chapters 5, 6, and 12, is filled with Web page descriptions and addresses. Be warned that Web addresses change often. The sites listed in these chapters are included in the Web version of

A Journalist's Guide to the Internet and will be updated regularly. The address is:

reporter.umd.edu

TELEPHONE DIRECTORIES

The phone book and directory assistance are the most basic of newsroom resources, but they have their limitations, namely geographic. If you do not know the city or town of the person you are trying to track down, directory assistance is of no assistance at all. And if you cannot identify a county or metropolitan area, the phone book is equally useless. But electronic telephone directories on the Internet provide the power of computing. Instead of searching through one county phone book at a time looking for the home phone number of a source, Internet phone directories allow you to search any geographic region, even the entire country, at the same time. Some good directories include:

Switchboard: www.switchboard.com
Yahoo! People Search: www.yahoo.com/search/people

Here is how they work, using Switchboard as the example. Say you are trying to track down this guy named Christopher Callahan. You know he lives in the northern part of Virginia, but do not have a street address, town, or even a county. Using the Go Directly to a Site method outlined in Chapter 2, type in the switchboard address. Then, input as much information as you have (you need at least a last name). The ease of finding names is dependent in part on the unusualness of the person's last name. If all you have to find your source is the last name *Smith,* forget it. But in our example here, you have my first and last name and the region. Our first attempt at "Christopher Callahan" in Virginia turns up no results. But remember, a person may not be listed by his or her full first name. When we try "Chris Callahan," we get six "hits" back. We can quickly eliminate "Christina" and "Christine" because we know we are looking for a Christopher. Of the other four, only one—"Christoph A Callahan"—is in northern Virginia, and that turns out to be the one you are seeking.

Remember that the computer is dumb; it is only going to find what is out there, precisely as the information is listed. Because the phone book lists me as Christoph instead of Christopher (I guess my name is too long for the phone company), you would never have found me unless you entered an abbreviated form. Sometimes it may be necessary to use only an initial, or perhaps just the last name. And if it is an unlisted number, that means it is unlisted on the Internet, too. These electronic directories also can be used to find businesses under yellow page sections and E-mail addresses.

CRISSCROSS DIRECTORIES

The computing power of Internet phone directories is seen in full when used as a crisscross directory: that is, when you have an address, but do not know who lives there or the phone number. Crisscross, or reverse, directories have been used in newsrooms for years when trying to track down neighbors, or when a deadline is fast approaching and a major story is breaking far from the newsroom. They are, however, quite expensive, and many smaller newsrooms and most college papers cannot afford them.

Because Internet phone directories are simply large databases that include names, addresses, and phone numbers, it is simple to "reverse" the search. That is, search on an address without a name. But many of the largest Internet phone directories have eliminated the crisscross function, citing privacy concerns. At least one of the major directories, however, continues its crisscross function. The address for Four 11 is:

www.four11.com

Once at the Four 11 site, click on "Telephone" under Directories on the left side of the page, then type in an address. Let's try an example. Say we are trying to figure out who lives at 930 Jaysmith Street in Great Falls, Virginia. Typing in the full address gets no results (remember, computers are dumb). Now we will try the address without the word *street*. That search successfully gets us the name and phone number.

Because addresses in the United States are sequential, with even numbers on one side of the street and odd on the other, we can guess at the likely addresses of neighbors. In this case, 928 and 932 Jaysmith Street likely will be the next-door neighbors, and 929 and 931 Jaysmith likely will be neighbors across the street.

Another type of reverse directory searches using the phone number to find the person and address. This could be useful when trying to verify a phone number or check numbers called by a public official. A good phone number reverse directory is maintained by Database America at:

www.databaseamerica.com/html/gpfind.htm

MAPS

Like phone books, street maps are among the most basic of reporting tools. Squinting over the tiny print of a map in a darkened car is a not-so-glamorous, but oft-repeated scene as reporters race to the scene of a fire or try to find an obscure meeting place. Driving and reading a map at the same time is a useful—albeit dangerous—art form. Internet mapping programs, however, allow you to type in a specific address and get an instant print out of the area. They also allow you to "zoom in" and "zoom out" on the area in question. Reporters about to leave for a story can reduce the inevitable getting-lost time by printing out two maps: a wide view that shows the location along with the nearest familiar thoroughfare, and a close-up that shows every side street and cul-de-sac and even maps out where on a block the address is located. Among the better mapping programs available are:

MapBlast: www.mapblast.com
Yahoo! Maps: maps.yahoo.com/yahoo

The two maps in Figures 4.1 and 4.2 from Yahoo! Maps give different views of 930 Jaysmith Street, Great Falls, Virginia, and the surrounding area.

ROLODEX SOURCES

The Rolodex is a mainstay of the newsroom. Every city desk, and the individual desks of all good reporters, hold a well-worn flip-card index filled

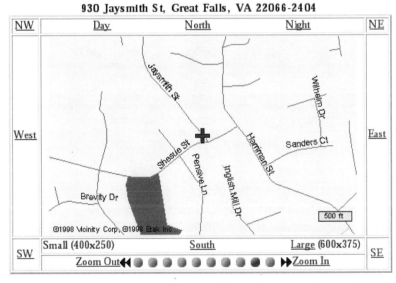

FIGURE 4.1   Text and artwork copyright © 1994–98 Yahoo! Inc. All Rights Reserved. Yahoo! and the Yahoo! logo are trademarks of Yahoo! Inc. Maps Copyright Etak, Inc. 1984–1998. All Rights Reserved.

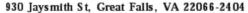

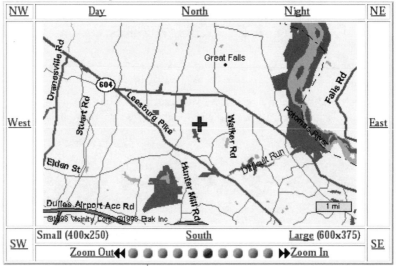

[**Driving Directions** | **Locate Businesses** NEW! | New Address | Print Preview | Mail a Map]

FIGURE 4.2   Text and artwork copyright © 1994–98 Yahoo! Inc. All Rights Reserved. Yahoo! and the Yahoo! logo are trademarks of Yahoo! Inc. Maps Copyright Etak, Inc. 1984–1998. All Rights Reserved.

with names and numbers of sources. There is no replacement for a reporter's personalized Rolodex, but, on the Internet, there are several sites that are designed to help reporters find expert sources that may add to your source list.

ProfNet, a service run by PR Newswire, has a list of 2,000 experts on a variety of topics, searchable by keyword at:

www.profnet.com/ped.html

Another experts database is put together by the National Press Club at:

npc.press.org/sources

It is searchable by category, organization or keyword.

Kitty Bennett, news researcher at the *St. Petersburg Times,* has compiled a one-stop Web site for reporters looking for expert sources on deadline. Her site is available at:

sunsite.unc.edu/slanews/internet/experts.html

FREEDOM OF INFORMATION ACT

Journalists and others can file written requests under the Freedom of Information Act to pry information from uncooperative federal bureaucrats and agencies. Although it is used as a last resort by reporters, because of the response times that often drag into years, it remains a powerful tool of investigative reporting. Unfortunately, some reporters—myself included— haven't been as aggressive in filing FOIA requests, in part because of the time delays and in part because it requires writing a formal letter citing the appropriate aspects of the law and finding the right people to send it to. Well, our friends at the Reporters Committee for Freedom of the Press, the Arlington, Virginia–based nonprofit group devoted to aiding journalists in First Amendment battles for nearly 30 years, have put together an on-line version of a FOIA request, complete with a fill-in-the-blanks form and the addresses of the various FOIA offices. It is located at:

www.rcfp.org/foi_lett.html

Fill in the blanks with your specific information, print it out, and mail. As Jane Kirtley, executive director of the Reporters Committee for Freedom of the Press, writes: "The possibilities provided by the (Freedom of Information) Act are endless. All that is required is that journalists use it."

STATE OPEN MEETING AND PUBLIC RECORD LAWS

The Freedom of Information Act applies only to federal government agencies and records. State records and meetings are covered by individual public record and open meeting laws in each state. And the laws vary widely from state to state. Ideally, all reporters should have a copy of both laws at their disposal and know how to use them. But in the reality of overburdened newsrooms, few editors and even fewer reporters know the details of their open meeting and public records law, or even how to access them quickly.

Once again, the Reporters Committee for Freedom of the Press has provided an invaluable service to all journalists by putting on the Internet the full text of its comprehensive "Tapping Officials' Secrets" guides. These guides, one for each state, outline each law, including what information is public, how to obtain the information, and how to appeal. The guides also detail how the law has been applied in the past. The Reporters Committee's state law guides are particularly valuable in the era of electronic records. The guides specify whether the state laws cover electronic records, whether reporters can demand records in electronic form, and whether electronic mail correspondence by public officials are covered under the statutes. Go to:

www.rcfp.org/tapping/index.cgi

STATE PUBLIC RECORDS REQUESTS

The student version of the Reporters Committee, the Student Press Law Center, has used the FOIA letter generator idea and created a similar site for state government public records requests for all 50 states. Select a state and the appropriate language for that state's open records law is automatically inserted into the letter. This is a tremendously powerful tool because both state and local government records must be requested under the state statutes. Go to:

www.splc.org/ltr_sample.html

VITAL RECORDS

Records such as birth certificates, marriage licenses, and other vital records are available only in paper form, but MedAccess provides a listing of how to write for those records in all 50 states. MedAccess is at:

www.medaccess.com

The Social Security Death Index is made available through Ancestry, Inc., a genealogical firm, at:

www.ancestry.com/ssdi/advanced.htm

MATH AID

Many people are drawn to journalism early in life in part because of the apparent lack of math. But math-challenged reporters soon find out that basic calculations—means, percent changes, per capita spending, margin of error—come up every day in the newsroom. Robert Niles has developed "Statistics

Every Writer Should Know," a user-friendly Web site that walks journalists through the minefield of mathematics. It is at:

nilesonline.com/stats

FAST FACTS

The Census Bureau's Statistical Abstract of the United States contains a wide range of statistics describing various social and economic aspects of the country. The latest version is available at:

www.census.gov/stat_abstract

Need to get your hands quickly on a thumbnail sketch of the demographics of a particular country? Look it up in the CIA World Factbook at:

www.odci.gov/cia/publications/nsolo/wfb-all.htm#TEXT

OTHER REFERENCE SOURCES

Other basic references available on the Internet include Bartlett's Familiar Quotations:

www.cc.columbia.edu/acis/bartleby/bartlett

Roget's Thesaurus:

humanities.uchicago.edu/forms_unrest/ROGET.html

And Webster's Dictionary:

work.ucsd.edu:5141/cgi-bin/http_webster

Now that we have covered some of the basic reporting tools on the Internet, let's plunge into some of the data-rich sites that can produce new stories and enrich old ones.

▶ 5

Top Data Sites
for News Stories

Much of what is found on federal, state, and local government Web sites is—from a journalistic perspective—garbage. They are filled largely with politicians stroking themselves and bureaucrats rationalizing their jobs. But between the puffery, reporters can find some of the best Web pages for news on government sites. In this chapter we will explore some of them. The focus here will be largely on the federal government because state, county, and municipal government sites are different in each locale. We will, however, explore local and state government sites in more depth in Chapter 8, on building an electronic beat.

FEDERAL GOVERNMENT SITES, GENERAL

Census Bureau

If every government agency used the Census Bureau's Web site as a model, the Net would be a much happier place for reporters. The Census Bureau site can be used by reporters for everything from checking a simple statistical fact in a story and adding demographic background to an article to forming the basis for groundbreaking trend stories. The main Census Bureau address is:

www.census.gov

The news section (www.census.gov/pubinfo/www/news.html) provides press releases—often embargoed—on the latest demographic, economic, and cultural changes and trends. The releases are linked to the raw statistics, which often are broken down to the county level and include contact numbers for census specialists.

But press releases are just the beginning. Click on the Search box or go directly to www.census.gov/main/www/srchtool.html to get detailed information on a state, county, city, or town from the latest census. Go to the U.S. Gazetteer (click on Place Search) and call up any of hundreds of different variables on your community, from the number of Eskimos to the time people leave for work to the number of bathrooms in the average home. Or click Map to get a tailored map of your community, with dozens of variables.

The Census Bureau also links users to the various state data centers around the country at:

www.census.gov/sdc/www

If you had access to only one data site on the Web, this may be the one. Spend some time getting to know its powerful and easily accessible tools. Figure 5.1 illustrates the home page of the U.S. Census Bureau, which is valuable for background information, daily stories, and trend pieces. Notice the "Population Clock," which provides up-to-the-second estimates of U.S. and worldwide populations.

FIGURE 5.1

BOX 5.1

Paul Overberg of USA Today *relies heavily on the U.S. Census Bureau Web site.*

The bad news—and good news—about most Census Bureau reports is that they come straight at you. Unlike most numbers analysts in Washington, census experts are reluctant to analyze and cautious when they do.

That's what it was like in April 1997 when the Bureau published its regular set of estimates of each state's age breakdown. A bureau tip sheet told us it was coming, but not when. When the data appeared on the bureau's Web site, it was noted with a one-paragraph announcement.

Each state's file carried eight categories of race and Hispanic data for each sex for each year of age up to 85. That made 1,360 data cells for each state, times six years, times 50 states, plus the District of Columbia.

You'd no sooner approach such a data pile without a plan than you would an interview with President Clinton. Our demographics reporter, Haya El Nasser, and I had talked about several ideas, and we had tried an old version of this data.

The one that worked best was showing where baby boomers had moved as they reached middle age in the 1990s. The states where they cluster are different than where they did in 1990, when they had different priorities, and the nation a different set of regional economic circumstances.

Without the Web and a spreadsheet, a deadline story like this was unthinkable. With both, it was a matter of a couple hours of sifting to pull out a customized slice of ages and measure its share in each state. Then El Nasser hit the phones with solid news that helped to draw quotes from demographers who were themselves curious about what we had found.

One unanticipated bonus: The Census Bureau had computed and tucked in each state's file its estimated median age for each year. Pulling these out, we saw that West Virginia had crept up on Florida and actually passed it to claim the oldest population in 1996. This surprised editors and became a nice paragraph for the story's roundup of trends.

Federal Register

Every business day the federal government publishes a book that details every new regulation, proposed rule, announced hearing, and every other administrative action taken by the executive branch of government the previous day. The Federal Register, however, traditionally has been used only by Beltway bureaucrats. Now the Register is on-line and searchable by keyword, giving local reporters around the country the power to find out how federal government executive branch decisions are affecting their communities. Take a look at the leads of these stories, which were produced by University of Maryland students writing for the College of Journalism's Capital News Service public affairs reporting program. The genesis of each story came from obscure references in the Federal Register found in a single Internet search.

Melissa Corley's story was published in the Baltimore *Sun,* and other Maryland papers:

> *Sunbathers perched atop military firing targets in the Chesapeake Bay have prompted the Navy to push for tougher restrictions at the firing range, Pentagon officials said.*

Nicole Gill's article ran in the *Washington Times* and the Baltimore *Sun:*

> *SILVER SPRING—Two dozen historic buildings at the Walter Reed Army Medical Center are in such disrepair that the Pentagon is considering ripping down or selling off the structures.*
>
> *The Forest Glen Annex buildings, which served as a women's finishing school from the late 19th century until World War II, go largely unused and are too expensive to maintain, Army officials say.*

Steven Kreytak wrote this feature that appeared in several newspapers on Maryland's Eastern Shore:

> *They have prowled the depths of the Chesapeake Bay since dinosaurs roamed the earth, but for the last 30 years the shortnose sturgeon have been on the verge of extinction.*
>
> *In fact, up until this year, scientists believed there were none left in the bay. But fishermen found three shortnose sturgeons in their nets in April, renewing the hopes of scientists and environmentalists alike.*
>
> *And now, government scientists are launching a study they hope will show that the three shortnose sturgeons found this spring represent the remnants of a Chesapeake Bay population and not just stray visitors from the nearby Delaware River.*

Sunny Kaplan wrote a series of features for the *Sun* on historic sites placed on the National Register of Historic Places.

The Federal Register is probably one of the worst-looking and clunkiest sites out there. And reporters have to poke through quite a bit of bureaucratese to find the nuggets of news. But it is also one of the most valuable Internet sites for producing original local news. Give it a try by looking at the last few months of the Federal Register, using the town or county that you cover as keywords. Other good keywords include local waterways, utilities, companies, military installations, and hospitals.

The Federal Register, dating back to 1995 on the Internet, is located within the Government Printing Office site. Go there directly at:

www.access.gpo.gov/su_docs/aces/aces140.html

CONGRESS

The Thomas site, named for Thomas Jefferson, includes full texts of all U.S. House and Senate legislation, the *Congressional Record* and Index, E-mail addresses for lawmakers, legislators' directories, committee assignments, the U.S. Constitution, Declaration of Independence, congressional ethics manual, and other resources. This site also has jumping off points to the Code of Federal Regulations and U.S. Code. It is located at:

thomas.loc.gov

The Thomas congressional site (see Figure 5.2) allows local reporters to monitor their legislators' work in Washington.

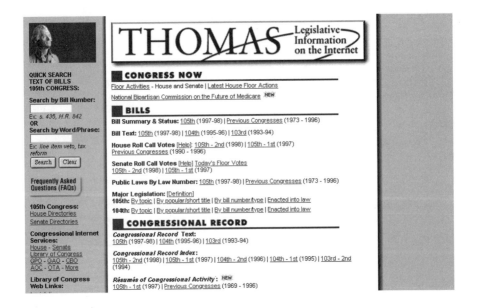

FIGURE 5.2

AIR TRAFFIC SAFETY

The Federal Aviation Administration offers a series of databases that includes government reports on aviation accidents, near collisions, traffic and capacity statistics, and other safety reports. The safety data is available at:

nasdac.faa.gov/safety_data

Landings, an extensive commercial aviation site, includes a searchable database of aircraft registration. Go to

www.landings.com

and click on Search.

TOXIC DATA

The Right-to-Know Network makes available the government's Toxic Release Inventory, which enables reporters to pinpoint toxic emissions from specific plants. It is searchable by company or geographic location and details the type and quantity of toxic emissions. RTK Net includes other environmental databases. It is located at:

rtk.net

GOVERNMENT DOCUMENTS

The Government Printing Office provides the federal budget, congressional bills, presidential documents, the Federal Register, the Congressional Record, the U.S. Government Manual, and other government documents the day of publication. It is located at:

www.access.gpo.gov/su_docs/dbsearch.html

AUDITS

Each major agency of the federal government has an inspector general's office that conducts investigations and audits of the department and federal programs that the agency oversees. This site, located at:

www.ignet.gov

brings you to IG reports throughout the federal government.

CONGRESSIONAL INVESTIGATIONS

The General Accounting Office (GAO), the investigative arm of Congress, has new reports available on the Internet within days of their release. GAO reports help background issues for enterprise stories. The agency is located at:

www.gao.gov

LIBRARY OF CONGRESS

This system includes brief descriptions and the status of all bills and resolutions in the U.S. Congress, past and present. It also includes the Library of Congress card catalog, which is useful for identifying potential expert sources for a particular topic. It also has select Congressional Research Service reports, which, like GAO reports, are useful for backgrounding issues. Reach the Library of Congress at:

lcweb.loc.gov

MEDICAL DATABASE

Medline, a database of more than 9 million references to articles published in nearly 4,000 medical journals, is made available through the National Library of Medicine at the National Institutes of Health. Reach Medline at:

www.ncbi.nlm.nih.gov/PubMed

OTHER FEDERAL AGENCIES

The Villanova Center for Information Law and Policy provides a Web site to jump off to any federal agency. It is at:

www.law.vill.edu/fed-agency

POLITICS

Federal Campaign Finances

If reporters had heroes, Tony Raymond would be mine. Raymond left his post at the Federal Election Commission and created what may be the most

BOX 5.2

Bill Loving, computer-assisted reporting editor at the Minneapolis Star Tribune, *explains how he combined a tip from an Internet discussion group, Web data, and a spreadsheet analysis to develop a story on tornado patterns in Minnesota.*

The Minneapolis *Star Tribune*'s computer-assisted reporting story on tornadoes in June 1997 is a good example of the power of the Internet as a reporting tool: The story idea itself actually originated in an Internet discussion group, then was carried out with data downloaded from a Web site. This also shows the most powerful application of the Internet for journalists, in my opinion: access to searchable or downloadable databases on-line.

Sometime in 1996 I noticed a message posted to NICAR-L, the E-mail discussion group hosted by National Institute for Computer-Assisted Reporting, from a reporter who had technical questions about converting historical tornado data into maps. I took note of the existence of the tornado data, which was stored at a Web site, and put it on my list of future story ideas.

In the spring of 1997, as Minnesota's tornado season approached, I went back to that Web site, maintained by the Storm Prediction Center at the University of Oklahoma (www.nssl.uoknor.edu/~spc/), clicked my way to the on-line archive section, and downloaded the data on Minnesota tornadoes from 1950 through 1995. (There are tables for each of the 50 states, plus one for the entire country.) The download was quite simple: The data table was stored as a compressed "zip" file, which I downloaded in Netscape Navigator simply by clicking on a link to the file. I also downloaded the accompanying record layout file.

After unzipping the data file with WinZip, I opened it into the Microsoft Excel spreadsheet program. Voila: In a few minutes I had an Excel table of 858 reported tornadoes, including the dates and times, intensity ratings, damage levels, deaths and injuries, and, best of all, the latitude and longitude coordinates of the tornadoes' paths. That meant that the tornadoes could indeed be mapped with GIS mapping software, which takes databases containing geographic location fields and converts them to maps.

I went to the *Star Tribune* science editor, Josephine Marcotty, and suggested a story on tornadoes for our weekly Science page. She was excited about the idea, and assigned it to science writer Jim Dawson and scheduled it for early June, the beginning of Minnesota's peak season for twisters.

Because I knew I would want to group and sum the tornado data by various measures, rather than just sorting and filtering, I imported the Excel table into Microsoft Access database software, which I find easier and more powerful for such operations. I exported the resulting summary data back into Excel and created some charts for the reporter on most com-

(Continued)

BOX 5.2 *Continued*

mon dates and times-of-day for tornadoes, and so on. Then I exported the
data into Arcview, a mapping program, which was able to read the latitude and longitude data and plot the
location of each tornado on a map of
Minnesota.

The maps and several charts
were published on the Science page as
part of a package of stories on tornado
season, just a couple of weeks after the
idea was first proposed.

reporter-friendly and journalistically powerful site on the Internet. Raymond, working at the nonprofit Center for Responsive Politics, is the archi-
tect of FECInfo, a site where thousands of FEC documents are collected and
presented in searchable forms. Through FECInfo, reporters can find out how
much money their local congressional or Senate candidates spent on a particular race or how much money they raised. But that's only the beginning.
FECInfo allows reporters to easily determine who in their community are
the biggest campaign contributors, which communities give the most
money, and which local special-interest groups are the most generous with
their campaign dollars. Reach FECInfo at:

www.tray.com/fecinfo

At the American University's (AU) School of Communication, Wendell
Cochran and his students provide a Web site where reporters can download
the full campaign finance documents to conduct their own, more detailed
analyses. AU's campaign data site is available at:

www.soc.american.edu/campfin

State Campaign Finances

State campaign finance sites are slowly coming to the Internet, but because
some states do not even require politicians to file their forms electronically,
it will be a while before Web campaign finance sites become the norm. Investigative Reporters and Editors and the National Institute for Computer-
Assisted Reporting are working on state campaign finance projects. Keep up
to date on what is happening in your state at:

www.campaignfinance.org

BOX 5.3

Ernie Slone, computer-assisted reporting editor at the Orange County Register, *explains how he used the Internet to figure out how tax dollars are spent.*

Promise that it will last; but in this world nothing is certain but death and taxes.
—Benjamin Franklin

The world hasn't changed much since Franklin wrote those words two centuries ago. Come April and many of your neighbors will be thinking about that check they will have to send off to Uncle Sam. And you can bet they will grouse about it—with good reason.

Federal, state, and local taxes in 1997 claimed 38 percent of the income of a median two-earner U.S. family (making $54,910), up from 37.3 percent in 1996. That is more than they spend on food (8.9 percent), clothing (3.7 percent), housing (15.3 percent), and transportation (6.6 percent), combined. The tax burden, adjusted for inflation, is at historic highs.

While reporters and editors often give the average Jane or José in-depth consumer analysis on how much they pay for meat, or autos, or mortgages, we seldom tell that typical family what they are getting for the $22,521 in taxes they spent in 1997. Too often we lapse into the uninformative cliché: how long was the line at the post office or why did you wait until the last minute?

By pulling data from the Internet, or getting it via E-mail, you can penetrate the unknown, telling your readers with enlightening accuracy how much they spend on federal taxes, how much comes back to their area, and who benefits. You also can tell them how good a job the government is doing in catching those who dodge their responsibilities.

Here is how the *Orange County Register* tells those stories to its readers:

Federal Spending Data

Each year in mid-April the Census Bureau posts Consolidated Federal Fund reports, basically how and where the government spent its money for the fiscal year. The data is available yearlong on the Internet, a great resource for stories about such issues as the decline of military spending. But here's an insider's tip: By contacting the Census folks in advance you can get them to E-mail or express mail you the latest detailed data on your area, usually in early April, plus the state and national summaries. Then, when April 15 rolls around, you are ready to print or broadcast a tax profile with the latest information. The address is

www.census.gov/govs/www

Click on Federal Government Data. (You will note that the site also offers detailed data on state tax collections, state government finances, etc.)

To make sense of the numbers you will need an understanding of relational databases, which can take one list and match it up with another. (This is a good early-learning project to begin developing those skills.) When you download the data, make sure you get two reference files to convert codes in the detail data files to more descriptive text:

- The Program Identification File contains program identification codes and names.
- The Agency File contains federal agency identification codes and names.

The dollars include grants to local government, salaries and wages of

(Continued)

BOX 5.3 *Continued*

federal employees in your area, direct payments to individuals for programs such as Social Security, and federal procurement contracts.

The Register also adds payments Orange County receives for Medicaid and Aid to Families with Dependent Children, which don't show up in the Census numbers. Those amounts are readily available from the two federal agencies.

The data is only the beginning, leading you to fascinating stories behind the numbers. In 1996 the federal government spent $215,265 in our county to bury veterans, and $435,582 for a "talent search" to find poor kids who might make it in college. We told stories of individuals, how a disabled veteran's life has been turned around thanks to government grants and how a professor is stretching $13,510 in research funds to try to save endangered forests in Southern California.

It will make your readers and viewers wonder if too much money is spent on some things, and not enough on others.

Federal Tax Data

In 1996 Orange County sent $15.9 billion to Washington, but got back only about $10 billion, one of the biggest deficits among California counties. (No wonder we had that bankruptcy thing.)

To find out how much your county or city is shipping to the feds contact the Tax Foundation.

The foundation is a nonprofit, nonpartisan policy research organization that has monitored fiscal issues at the federal, state, and local levels since 1937. Its on-line site is at

www.taxfoundation.org

The site provides dozens of detailed tables, listing tax burden by state, how much a typical family pays, when

"tax freedom" day occurs each year, and so forth. But for the really detailed information on your local area, you need to contact the foundation and request those numbers. Staffers are very responsive, but typically need a couple of days to send it.

In 1996 each of our county's 2.6 million residents sent an average of $6,000 to Uncle Sam, a tenth of all the federal tax dollars collected in the Golden State.

Tax Enforcement

If we are so generous, that must mean few Orange Countians are fudging on their taxes, right? Don't tell that to the IRS. In 1996 Southern California residents were audited at the second-highest rate in the country. Who got audited more, you ask? Those reckless devils across the desert in Las Vegas, of course.

But while auditors looked very closely at our records, federal prosecutors took a different view. The federal district that includes our county was among the lowest in the country for referring, prosecuting, and convicting tax criminals, and the few who were convicted received only 8.3 months in the federal slammer, compared with a national average of double that term. (When we wrote that story the federal prosecutor complained that he would like to pursue more cheaters, but doesn't have the staff.)

You can tell your readers and viewers how your area rates on audits and tax enforcement by accessing the data from Syracuse University's Transactional Records Access Clearinghouse at

trac.syr.edu

While the data is there, free for the taking, none of these stories will get done without planning and initiative. Remember that other quote from old Ben Franklin: "God helps them that help themselves."

Other Political Sources

Harvard University's Kennedy School of Government provides a good general directory of political resources at:

ksgwww.harvard.edu/~ksgpress/opinhome.htm

Congressional Quarterly's American Voter is another excellent source at:

voter96.cqalert.com

The Gallup Organization has its polling data available on-line at:

www.gallup.com

And both the Democrats (www.democrats.org) and Republicans (www.rnc.org) have well-established sites. The partisan sites are important not only to get information on the parties and individual candidates, but to analyze how politicians are using the Internet as part of the campaigning process.

BUSINESS

Securities and Exchange Commission

The Securities and Exchange Commission (SEC) Edgar database is a repository for documents filed at the SEC. Reporters can access 10Ks, 13Ds, proxies, and other vital corporate documentation. It is probably the most important site for business reporters, but also is valuable for local reporters who want to go beyond press release reporting on the utilities and big employers in their circulation area. The Edgar database was one of the first on the Web to provide full-text documents, and remains one of the most journalistically powerful. Find it at:

www.sec.gov/edaux/searches.htm

State Corporate Records

The Prospector provides links to secretaries of state offices, which regulate corporations and charities. Find the Prospector at:

w3.uwyo.edu/~prospect/secstate.html

Nonprofits

GuideStar provides financial data from Internal Revenue Service 990 filings 501(c)(3) charities, searchable by name, town, or type of organization. Go to:

www.guidestar.org

The Internet Nonprofit Center allows users to search for all nonprofit organizations by name or by zip code. Go to:

www.nonprofits.org/library/gov/irs/search_irs.shtml

Workplace Safety

The Occupational Safety and Health Administration provides a database of workplace inspection reports, violations, and fines, searchable by institution. It is available at:

www.osha.gov/oshstats

Other Business Sites

Hoover's, Inc. offers a searchable database that provides useful details on many companies. Each company listing includes Web and mail addresses, a thumbnail profile, competitors, stock quotes, the company's press releases, news stories mentioning the company, SEC filings, and annual reports. Hoover's is located at:

www.hoovers.com

Business-related press releases are available through Business Wire at:

www.businesswire.com

and PR NewsWire at:

www.prnewswire.com

LEGAL

U.S. Circuit Courts of Appeals

The U.S. Circuit Courts of Appeals are by far the most undercovered courts in the country. Big federal cases are covered aggressively when in U.S. District Court, but often disappear when they are appealed and go to the next level—the Circuit Courts. That is in large part because the Circuit Courts often are out of the newspapers' reach. For instance, the 4th Circuit Court, which covers federal appeals from Maryland, is in Richmond, Virginia, about three hours south of Baltimore. Newspapers traditionally have relied on local wire coverage, but the wires usually only cover the court sporadically. Now, the geographic problem no longer exists because the full-text opinions of all 11 Circuit Courts of Appeals are available on the Internet. The Emory University School of Law has links to the rulings at:

www.law.emory.edu/FEDCTS

A quick check each day of your Circuit Court can provide good breaking stories that the competition doesn't have. How many stories? Well, Capital News Service student reporters covering the 4th Circuit Court via the Web for Maryland daily newspapers had eight articles published by a wide variety of Maryland daily newspapers over the course of one semester (12 weeks). Their stories ranged from a murder-for-hire death sentence appeal and an illegal alien smuggling case to an age discrimination suit and a claim by a federal scientist that his colleagues were trying to destroy his reputation.

Supreme Court

While the wires cover Supreme Court rulings much more comprehensively than they cover the Circuit Courts, you may want to expand on coverage of high court rulings that come from your area. The Cornell University Law School has full-text U.S. Supreme Court decisions available the day of release at:

supct.law.cornell.edu/supct

The Cornell Law site has opinions dating back to 1990. For older Supreme Court cases (opinions from 1937 through 1975), go to:

www.fedworld.gov/supcourt/index.htm

State Appellate Courts

Robert Ambrogi of legal.online has linked state appellate court sites. Go to

www.legalonline.com/courts.htm

to see if your state appellate court rulings are available on-line.

Legalonline.com also provides links to fee-based systems that provide state court opinions and to the few U.S. District Courts and U.S. Bankruptcy Courts that provide opinions on the Internet.

Securities Cases

The Stanford University School of Law has started to make available full-text complaints, summaries, and briefs on securities class action complaints. See the Stanford site at:

securities.stanford.edu

Law Library

The U.S. House of Representatives Internet Law Library is a terrific reference for legal and general assignment reporters alike. It provides the full text of all federal laws plus state and territorial laws, international treaties and laws, laws of other nations, and hyperlinks to other legal references. See the House Internet Law Library at:

law.house.gov

Legal Directory

West's Legal Directory contains thumbnail profiles of more than 800,000 U.S. law firms and attorneys. It is searchable by name, state, town, type of law, college attended, and other factors. Go to:

www.wld.com

Other Legal Resources

FindLaw provides links to a wide range of material helpful to legal reporters, from state and local bar associations to state laws. Go to:

www.findlaw.com

STATE AND LOCAL GOVERNMENTS

The Web sites of some state and local agencies and legislative bodies are rich in documents and data, while others remain close to useless. Take some time to review what is available on your state and local government sites. And even if you leave disappointed with what is available on your state's Web sites, keep an eye out for future improvements. Like everything else on the Web, the content on state and local government sites is changing with each passing day.

State Governments

To find a state site, use GlobalComputing's links at:

www.globalcomputing.com/states.html

Also, many states can be reached at www.state.??.us, with the question marks standing for the two-initial state abbreviation.

BOX 5.4

Penny Loeb, senior editor at U.S. News & World Report, *explains how a state government database on the Internet helped her nail down a story about coal mining.*

"Shear Madness" was the headline for my investigation of a kind of coal mining in West Virginia known as mountaintop removal. The mines literally take up to 500 feet off the top to get at multiple coal seams. Much of the top of the mountain ends up in the valleys below. During the process, residents' homes are damaged by blasting, and their wells dry up. Even entire communities are being eliminated.

When I started the project, I asked state environmental officials how much of the mountains were being mined. They couldn't tell me. No acreage seemed to exist in paper reports. Every large surface mine has several permits, and these do have acreage. But nobody seemed to have added up the acreage.

I was going to accept what state officials told me. We were using our own estimations from flying over the mines. These were confirmed by the state official who flew with us. We said about 15 percent of the mountains in southern West Virginia had been mined.

A lot of lucky things happened to me on this story. And this is one. About a month before publication, I was looking at the maps of coal mines on the Web site for the state Division of Environmental Protection. (This agency has one of the best Web sites I've seen for a government.) I thought I could download a map for our art department. In trying to open the map after downloading, I noticed I had gotten a .dbf file. I like those. I opened it up. It was all the individual permits, with acreage. All I had to do was add up the acreage for surface mines. It came to about 323,000 acres. My editor liked square miles better: 512 square miles. Unfortunately the database couldn't count the number of mountains being cut off.

City Governments

Web sites for many city governments can be found by using a similar pattern. For cities, try:

www.ci.xxx.zz.us

The xxx stands for a city abbreviation (sf for San Francisco, nyc for New York), and the zz is the two-initial state abbreviation.

We will get into state and local government sites in more detail in Chapter 8, which explores creating an electronic beat system with the Web. But before we get there, let's look at how we can access the work of other journalists and use that to help in our own reporting.

▶ 6

On-line News: Electronic Publications

GROWTH OF ON-LINE NEWSPAPERS

Shortly after the birth of the World Wide Web came a flood of on-line news publications as newspapers and magazines—fearful of becoming anachronisms—rushed to publish on-line. At the beginning of 1998, there were more than 3,600 newspapers on the Internet, according to the *American Journalism Review*. What the on-line publishing world will look like 10 years from now, five years from now, or even next year is unclear as publications struggle to figure out how to best utilize the uniqueness of the medium and make money at it. Some predict that on-line news publications, tailored to individual readers, will grow exponentially in the near future, eventually taking the place of the traditional daily newspaper in our culture. Others say the on-line world will soon shrink as news outlets fail to turn a profit, leaving just a handful of the big on-line products along with smaller specialty publications. While the future of on-line journalism is murky, what is clear is that the Internet will continue to be a valuable reporting resource for traditional print and broadcast journalists. Let's explore how on-line news products can help you and your news publications.

LOCAL BREAKING NEWS

Reporters and editors keep an eye on the Associated Press local wire throughout the day as a way to check on new breaking stories and to compare facts to their own staff stories. Many daily newspaper reporters have access to the news wires right on their desktop computers. But others can access the wires only through editors' terminals, and most weekly newspapers and some smaller dailies and college papers don't even get a wire service.

The AP does not provide its stories on the Web, but many newspapers that belong to the AP cooperative do publish wire stories on their Web sites. For instance, to find the local AP news from Florida, you could go to *Tampa Bay Online*. The *Hartford Courant* has the AP Connecticut wire on its on-line product.

The AP has linked on its home page the local wires used at various papers around the country. Go to:

wire.ap.org

and you will find links to newspapers around the country that carry local AP news on their Web pages. These stories cannot be published without purchasing AP service, but reporters can refer to these stories throughout the day to compare coverage of a spot story or to keep up with other breaking news in the area.

REGIONAL AND STATEWIDE NEWSPAPERS

Most parts of the country have a dominant regional or statewide newspaper. In Massachusetts, it is the *Boston Globe*. Illinois has the *Chicago Tribune*. In California, it is the *Los Angeles Times*. Keeping close tabs on the dominant regional paper allows local reporters to compare their coverage to the larger regional competition and can provide story ideas that can be localized. In the past, those papers often were not easily accessible in the far corners of a state until later in the day or even the following day. Now they can be accessed instantly via the Internet, in some cases before the printed version even hits the streets. And nearly every major metropolitan daily newspaper in the country had a Web site by 1997.

There are several Web pages that link to newspapers around the country. Two of the best are the *American Journalism Review's* NewsLink at

www.ajr.org/news.html

and NewsCentral at

www.all-links.com/newscentral

NewsLink provided hyperlinks to 3,622 newspapers around the world in 1998. NewsCentral had links to more than 3,500 newspapers. To get to NewsCentral's 1,123 U.S. newspapers, listed by state, go directly to:

www.all-links.com/newscentral/northamerica/unitedstates.html

NewsLink and NewsCentral also can help you find smaller publications in your region.

NATIONAL PUBLICATIONS

Reading major publications such as the *New York Times* and the *Washington Post* often can provide story ideas that can be localized for your newspaper. Also, following publications that excel in coverage of your issue beat can provide you with story ideas and important background information. For instance, political reporters may want to keep up with the *Washington Post*. Reporters covering high technology issues may want to read the *San Jose Mercury News*. Higher education reporters may want to look at the *Boston Globe*. Reporters covering elderly issues might look to the *St. Petersburg Times*. You also may want to keep tabs on the work of a specific reporter who is well known for covering your issue. Use AJR's NewsLink or NewsCentral to find the newspapers you want to track.

The on-line versions of *USA Today* (see Figure 6.1) and the *New York Times* (see Figure 6.2) reflect the look of their printed counterparts.

OUT-OF-STATE PUBLICATIONS

There are local stories that have strong out-of-town connections. The best example is that of a high-profile official in one location being considered for a job, or hired for a job, in another location. For instance, the president of Ohio State University left to become president of Brown University in Providence, Rhode Island, and the president of the University of Maryland at College Park, William Kirwan, was hired to take over the Ohio State post. The Kirwan story was big news not only in Maryland, where he was leaving, but in Ohio. And papers in both towns were competing for the story before it was officially announced. Just a few years ago, a Maryland reporter would not have easy access to the *Columbus Dispatch* and other Ohio papers covering the Kirwan story, just as the Ohio reporters would have a tough time getting hold of that day's Baltimore *Sun*. But now those papers can be easily accessed on the Web.

TRADE AND SPECIALTY PUBLICATIONS

Daily, weekly, and monthly newsletters and magazines that specialize in a single topic are valuable tools for daily beat reporters. The best of these

Mike Tyson faces $22 million lawsuit for alleged abuse of two women

3/10/98 - Updated 4:44 PM ET

Inside
Nationline
Stocks
Scores
Baseball
NFL
NCAA
Books
Hot Sites
Web tech
Politics
Opinion
Travel
States
Lotteries
Snapshots

Search
Our site
Newspaper
Archives
Yellow pages

Shopping
Marketplace
BookStore
click here

Classifieds
Autos
Jobs
Homes
Apts
Start/Own
a Business

Resources
Index
Feedback
What's Hot
The FAQ
Classline

About us
Terms of
service
Privacy
policy
Our brands
How to
advertise
How to
subscribe
Jobs at
USA TODAY

Dow industrials roll to new high

Blue-chip barometer closes above 8600 for first time; tech stocks rebound.

| MARKET REPORT | Dow ▲75.98 at | 8643.12 |
| Reload for indexes | Nasdaq ▲23.35 at | 1748.51 |

Imagine Winning a Mercury

Click Here!

Willey appears before grand jury

Former aide to be asked if she was urged to change story.

TODAY'S BEST BETS

A reporter's fight
USA TODAY's Cathy Hainer shares her experience.

Music Tuesday
Aretha Franklin
Queen of Soul shines on 'A Rose is Still a Rose.'

Eric Clapton
Quietly powerful 'Pilgrim' reveals singer's progress.

Listen Up
Reviews of Van Dyke Parks, 'Wedding Singer' music.

Books
Free book
Win a best seller from BarnesandNoble.com.

Terry Bisson
Award-winning author opens this month's series.

BookStore
Reviews, author chats plus online shopping discounts.

Marketplace
BarnesandNoble.com
Read the books that have won awards.

Bad Day at Work?

TOP NEWS

News

Herman investigation
Probe into alleged influence peddling by Labor Secretary extended two months.

JonBenet case
Child beauty queen's murder may go to grand jury soon, district attorney says.

Money

Dow Corning
Plaintiffs in breast implant case offer to settle for $3.8 billion.

Economy
Growth in Americans' productivity slowed at the end of 1997, Labor Dept. says.

Sports

NBA
Chicago Bulls, Miami Heat clash in Eastern Conference showdown

College basketball
North Carolina's Antawn Jamison top vote-getter for All-America team

Life

Sense arousal
Study reveals aromas that most appeal to women: Good & Plenty candy, baby powder.

Travel news
Egypt has become strikingly militarized to protect precious tourist industry.

Weather

Winter's bite returns
Cold east of the Rockies will make today feel like January; Midwest digs out.

FIGURE 6.1 © Copyright 1998 USA Today Online. Used by permission.

The New York Times

ON THE WEB

"All the News That's Fit to Print"   **Tuesday, March 10, 1998**   ● Weather

● **NATIONAL**

Bilingual Education Is Facing
Its Toughest Test in California

● **TECHNOLOGY**

California Internet Firm Tracked
Teens in Hacking of Pentagon

● **INTERNATIONAL UPDATE**

Hindu Nationalists Are Asked
To Form Government in India

Gore - Ch

U.S. and Russia Discuss Space Program

● **POLITICS UPDATE**

Aide, Who Charged
Clinton Advance, Is
Called to Grand Jury

● **INTERNATIONAL**

On a Garage Floor in
Kosovo, a Gruesome
Harvest by the Serbs

● **NEWS BY CATEGORY** ● **A.P. BREAKING NEWS** ● Arts & Leisure ● Automobiles ● Books ● Business ● Diversions ● Editorials ● Front Page
● Job Market ● Op-Ed ● Politics ● Real Estate ● Sports ● Technology ● Travel ● Web Specials ● Week in Review ● **FORUMS** ● **SEARCH**

Classifieds | Contents | Help | Low Graphics | Privacy Information | Services | Site Tour

Welcome. Please register. It's free in the U.S. and takes just a couple of minutes.

New York Times Home Delivery

News by Category

● International   ● Technology   ● Style

● National   ● CyberTimes   ● Arts

● Metro   ● Science   ● Obituaries

● Politics   ● Business   ● Today's Photos

● Sports

Continual Updates, 24 Hours a Day

News
◆ Breaking News from A.P.: updated every 10 minutes
◆ A.P. Network News, a five-minute audio newscast updated twice an hour

Weather
◆ Forecasts, maps and information from 1,500 cities, up to the minute

Sports
◆ Up-to-the-minute scores and summaries

Business
◆ Market quotes for stocks, options, and mutual funds

FIGURE 6.2   Copyright © 1998 The New York Times Company

55

special-interest publications cover stories in-depth, and often break news before the mass circulation newspapers and magazines. For instance, when I was covering defense issues in Washington, *Defense Week* was on my must-read list because it broke stories that affected my readers, and most of my readers were not subscribers to the pricey newsletter. Many of these publications are available on the Web. Some of the publications will make available only parts of stories, or full versions of only some of their stories, but even those sites are useful to reporters who can then get the full-text versions of the stories of particular interest.

To find the right publications for your beat, try MediaFinder, which offers searchable directories of newsletters and magazines. MediaFinder is located at:

www.mediafinder.com

NEWSPAPER ARCHIVES

A weakness of the Web is in accessing past newspaper stories. Most newspapers that have electronic archives charge a fee. *Washington Post* researcher Margot Williams created a Web site that details the costs of the various archives and how far back the articles go in many U.S. newspapers. It is located at:

sunsite.unc.edu/slanews/internet/archives.html

READING FOR BETTER WRITING

The best writers are voracious readers. That's because one of the best ways to improve your own writing is to critically read, analyze, and dissect the writing of others. The Web allows you to access some of the best newspaper writing around easily—style section features in the *Washington Post*, trend stories in the *New York Times*, sports takeouts in the *Boston Globe*—to help your own writing.

And for pure writing and reporting inspiration, read the full-text originals of the latest Pulitzer Prize winning work in every category from public service and spot news to editorial writing and criticism, starting with the 1997 winners. Go directly to the Pulitzer works at:

www.pulitzer.org

► 7

Strategic Searching

The last three chapters described specific Web sites that beat reporters can use in their daily reporting, but those represent just a tiny handful of the material available on the Internet. In this chapter we will explore how to find information on the Net when you do not have a specific Web address.

THINK STRATEGICALLY: DEVELOP A GAME PLAN

Commercial databases such as Nexis–Lexis have spoiled some of us. Those well-designed, carefully thought out systems allow us to punch in a few keywords, swiftly expand or contract the scope of a search if needed, and within moments have the material we are seeking. Unfortunately, the Internet does not allow us that luxury. Instead of a single method of searching, there are dozens of search engines and directories that not only seek out information in different ways but look at different Internet materials and present the search results in different forms. That creates serious problems for reporters on deadline, and makes searching the Internet a more complicated process than using a commercial database. That is why, before we start punching in keywords, we should develop a strategy for each search.

WHAT ARE YOU LOOKING FOR AND WHERE IS IT LIKELY TO BE?

At the start of every search, ask yourself two questions: "What information am I looking for?" and "Which institutions will likely have that information?" The first question seems self-evident, but really isn't. Do we really know—specifically—what we are seeking? Let's say we are writing a piece on drug use on college campuses. What specific information do we want? At the beginning of the story, we would need to find statistics on drug use on campuses to quantify the issue and to show whether it is a growing or waning problem. We probably would want to get the specific drug policies of the colleges of interest to our audience. And we would want to find experts who could talk about the cultural phenomenon and historical dimensions of campus drug use. These are three areas where the Internet likely can be helpful in our reporting, but it is unlikely that the information will all be in the same place. In effect, each question we have posed should be considered a distinct search. That is why it is so important to specify the information you are seeking.

Now that we have an idea of what we want, the next question we need to ask ourselves is, "Where would that information likely be?" At this point, we may simply not know, and will have to go straight to a search engine or Internet directory. But in many cases, time can be saved and results improved if we have some reasonable idea of where the information might be. In our campus drug example, the only credible sources of information for the drug statistics would be law enforcement agencies. We might start out with the FBI and work backward to the state police, then to the county, city, or campus police. For the drug policy of specific colleges, we would go directly to the logical sources— the colleges—and search within their Web sites for the written policies. And for the experts, we may either search again on the local university sites or on some of the expert databases discussed in Chapter 4.

GUESSING

Now that we have figured out where the information is likely to be, we still need to find those specific Web sites. Again, before jumping on a search engine and typing in those key words, let's try something else first. Guess. That's right, just guess at the address. With the information from Chapter 2, we should be able to find many large Web sites without ever touching a search engine.

We know from Chapter 2 that the domain name—the basic Web address— usually has three main parts, separated by dots. The first is often (but not always) www, which of course stands for the World Wide Web. The second is a series of letters that gives the Web address its uniqueness. This often is either the full name of the institution or the institution's abbreviation. The last part of the main address is that three-letter suffix that tells us whether it is from the world of academia (.edu), government (.gov), commerce (.com), and so on (see p. 18). Let's try this out with our campus drug example. If we are looking for the Federal Bureau of Investigation, a good guess for that address might be www.fbi.gov (www for World Wide Web, FBI for Federal Bureau of Investigation, and .gov because it is a government site). If we are looking for the University of Maryland, we would try www.umd.edu (umd for University of Maryland and edu because it is an academic institution). In both cases, we would have saved ourselves the time of a search because those addresses are correct. Go back to Chapter 5 and look at how many of the addresses you probably could have guessed at correctly.

Does this mean you should spend lots of time guessing at an address? Certainly not, but try at least one or two addresses that you think would be logical, especially for relatively big institutions. It will save you precious minutes on deadline.

WHAT TO DO WHEN YOU DON'T KNOW WHERE TO GO

The method of mapping out where information likely will be and then targeting that information is an efficient and effective way to get your hands on information quickly. But what if you don't have a clue about where to look? Let's try another example. Let's say we are about to launch into a news feature on racial diversity in U.S. newsrooms. We would want to first find statistics that both illustrate the racial inequities in the news workforce today and give a historical context. We would want to find any studies conducted about the impact of these inequities. We also would want to learn about efforts under way to correct the problem. And, ideally, we would like to get some expert sources who could speak authoritatively about the subject. But, unlike with the campus drug story, we really don't know where to turn. For this story, we will have to search the Internet using one of two tools: directories or search engines.

DIRECTORIES

Internet directories are straightforward hierarchical systems that group Web sites into categories and subcategories. To search for information, we would go from a very general group into more specific subgroups until we have reached the type of information sought.

Directories are excellent for casual users interested in broad, general topic areas. Reporters may want to try directories at the beginning of a big enterprise story on an unfamiliar topic.

The most popular of all directories is the Yahoo! site, located at:

www.yahoo.com

but many of the big search engines now include their own directories.

I have found, however, that for most reporting circumstances, directories are simply too broad. When looking for specific information, Web search engines usually are the better bet.

SEARCH ENGINES

Here's the lead on Internet search engines: There are many, they all search for different things, they all search in different ways, and they all produce different results. And the kicker? You can do the same search on every engine available and still not know if what you are looking for is somewhere on the Internet.

HOW SEARCH ENGINES WORK

To understand how to use search engines, we need to know a bit about how they work and why they are imperfect. Search engines are Web sites designed to help you find information on the Internet. Each search site works by compiling a database of information on Web sites. The search engine's database is compiled by robot programs that wander around the Web looking for sites to include in the engine's database. But each engine produces different—in many cases extraordinarily different—results on the same keyword search because of the differences in both what information is collected for the database and how that information is analyzed by the program. Some retrieve only the titles of Web pages (the brief description located above the tool bar in your software program), some record parts of the document, and others index the entire page.

Another problem is that there is no standard search method among the various engines. Some use upper and lower cases, others don't; some recognize articles, others do not. Not even all of the search engines use common Boolean connectors such as AND, NOT, and OR. What search engines do have in common is an attempt to present results of a search in order of importance, with the top results, or "hits," from a search representing the best matches to that particular search. It is like the computer equivalent of the inverted pyramid. But, of course, each search engine has its own idea of what is an ideal match. Some weigh the number of times the keywords are mentioned in a site. Others give value to *where* those keywords are mentioned in the document, giving more weight to keywords toward the top of a site.

HOW TO USE SEARCH ENGINES EFFECTIVELY

Your search will depend in large part on the search engine you have selected. But there are some basic concepts that should be implemented in all of your reporting searches.

Take Advantage of Basic Commands to Tailor a Search. Each search engine uses its own set of commands to narrow a search by combining words and phrases that are likely to appear in the document. Searching multiple sets of words and phrases makes your search much more specific. You can find the individual commands under a section called "tips," "help," or "search tips" on the main page of each engine.

Be Specific in Keyword Selection. Select specific search words and phrases over more general words and phrases (as long as you are confident the selected keywords are likely to appear in the sought-after documents). The goal should be to come up with keywords that are most likely to appear in the documents being sought while unlikely to appear in unrelated sites.

Be Precise in Keyword Selection. Search engines, like everything in the computer world, take things quite literally. For instance, the former managing editor of the *New York Times,* Eugene Roberts, is called Gene by many. But he often is referred to in print by his full first name. So a search of Roberts should include both the phrases "Gene Roberts" and "Eugene Roberts."

Review Results Top to Bottom. Most search engines display search results in some type of hierarchical order—from what they believe to be the best fits to your search query to the least likely fits. Therefore, that is how you should always review the search results—from top to bottom—paying much more attention to the first page or two of results.

Analyze the Addresses of Results. Once search results are returned, do not just start opening up the Web pages. First take a moment to analyze not only the brief description of the site, but, just as importantly, look at the Internet address. Is it a government, educational, commercial, or other kind of site? Can you tell if it is from a group that you know? A few moments spent looking at the Web addresses and descriptions can save precious minutes used in waiting to connect to the various sites.

THE MAJOR SEARCH ENGINES

There are lots of different search engines out there, all with their pluses and minuses. Let's take a quick look at some of the most popular engines, their basic search features, and where to find them. Your browser software already has built-in links to some of the most popular search engines.

Alta Vista. One of the largest and best search engines, Alta Vista creates its database by retrieving the full text of Web pages. Users can search for exact phrases by putting the words that appear together in quotes, such as "home brew" for a feature on beer brewing at home. It also allows users to search for sets of words that appear in the desired documents by using the + (plus) sign (for example, *brewing + beer*). Without a plus sign, the Alta Vista search engine reads a request for brewing beer as *brewing* OR *beer*. It also allows you to search for documents *without* a particular word or phrase with a – (minus) sign. Alta Vista searches are case sensitive (if you search on Journalism with a capital "J," you will not get journalism with a small "j"). Alta Vista also recognizes wildcards (*) to broaden a search. For example, the search term journali* would find sites with both the word *journalism* and *journalist*. The advanced search function on Alta Vista uses traditional Boolean search terms (ANDs, ORs, and NOTs) instead of the + and – signs, provides for specifying dates, and has other functions that make a search more powerful and directed. The search engine also allows users to search for specific words in a Web address and to search for specific links on other pages. Alta Vista presents results according to both how many search terms a page contains and where in the document they appear. Alta Vista displays its results with the page title, the first few lines of the document, the size of the document in bytes or kilobytes, and the page address. Go to:

www.altavista.digital.com

Infoseek. Like Alta Vista, Infoseek assumes the OR on basic searches with more than one keyword (*home brewing* is read as *home* or *brewing*). The + sign functions as the AND connector, and the quotation marks find that exact phrase. It too recognizes upper and lower case and has some advanced searching options that are worthwhile to learn if you use the engine regularly. Results are generated in order of frequency of search words found on a page. Infoseek results are presented much like Alta Vista's. Go to:

www.infoseek.com

HotBot. Created by the folks at *Wired* magazine, HotBot provides a user-friendly front that does not require remembering whether it uses + and – or Boolean connectors or other search commands. There are pull-down menus to help tailor searches, to specify how much detail is desired in the results, and how many results should be returned. Results are ranked by considering both frequency and whether the search words appear in the title. Go to:

www.hotbot.com

Excite. Excite sells itself not only as producing results based on key-words, but by finding ideas and concepts closely related to the key-words. Here's an illustration Excite offers:

Suppose you enter elderly people financial concerns in the query box. In addition to finding sites containing those exact words, the search engine will find sites mentioning the economic status of retired people and the financial concerns of senior citizens. Our search engine can figure out that relationships exist between words and concepts—that the term elderly people is related to senior citizens. It learns about related concepts from the documents themselves, and learns more from each new document it indexes.

Some say this works better in theory than practice; nevertheless, Excite is one of the most popular engines. It recognizes the "exact phrase in quotes" function seen on many search engines, but uses a slightly different version of the + and – system. In Excite, you must put the symbol in front of every word you want included in the search. For example, news-papers + california will retrieve only California. That search in Excite would have to look like this: +newspapers +california. The same is true for trying to exclude a word or phrase with a – sign. Excite also recognizes the Boolean terms, but this will "turn off" the concept function of the search engine, returning only traditional keyword matches. Go to:

www.excite.com

Lycos. Another early search engine that remains popular is Lycos. It employs +, –, and "...." to refine searches and provides an option to search for words in a Web title and for words within specific Web addresses. Lycos may not have as many bells and whistles as some of the others, but it remains a solid search engine. Go to:

www.lycos.com

WebCrawler. Popular because it was one of the first Web search engines and because it is owned by America Online, WebCrawler is straightfor-ward and easy to use with traditional Boolean connectors. It does not, however, have the power of most of the other major search engines. Go to:

www.webcrawler.com

Yahoo! Yahoo is a different animal from the other search engines. Its searches are based on a directory concept, and the indexes are done by people rather than automated. That means two things: The amount of material searchable on Yahoo is much smaller than standard search engines, but the results often will be much more on target. It is easy to use, and because of its accurate results it is ideal for simple, general searches. Yahoo presents its results in a series of categories and subcategories. For instance, a search of "college newspapers" generates the following category listing from Yahoo: *News and Media: Newspapers: College and University.* Click on that and a list of the various college newspapers is produced. Yahoo uses AND and OR connectors only and is not case sensitive. Get to Yahoo directly at:

www.yahoo.com

THE META-SEARCH ENGINES

These are programs designed to carry out a single search on a number of different search engines simultaneously and report the overall results. For instance, MetaCrawler, located at:

www.metacrawler.com

searches Alta Vista, Excite, Infoseek, Lycos, WebCrawler, and Yahoo! simultaneously. But the results are not as complete as individual searches on each engine, and the reporting can be a bit confusing.

Another multi-engine search tool, Inference Find, searches the same six search engines, but attempts to collate the results. It is at:

www.inference.com/infind

Metafind, at

www.metafind.com

searches Alta Vista, Excite, HotBot, Infoseek, PlanetSearch, and WebCrawler.

The main problem with the meta-search engines is you cannot refine a search as much as you can using a single engine.

WHICH SEARCH ENGINE IS FOR YOU?

With all of the imperfections and inconsistencies in search engines, which ones should you use? Well, just like some folks swear by Netscape and others use only Explorer for their Web browser, most Net veterans have their search engine favorites. And many of those opinions are based on their own limited anecdotal experiences and which engines they started to use when they first got on the Internet. But the bottom line is that by the late 1990s, no single search engine has emerged as being clearly superior, as we will see in a moment in some case studies. My suggestion is simple: After playing around a bit, pick one or two well-established search engines that you feel comfortable with, and then spend the time to learn the idiosyncrasies and specific search techniques of those engines. Remember, much more important than which search engine you use is carefully crafting your search terms.

You also may want to use different search tools for different reasons. For example, if you are looking for some general information on a topic, you may want to go to a directory-based search such as Yahoo! For a more tailored search, employ search engines.

To keep up with changes in the search engine field, check out Monash Information Services at:

www.monash.com/spidap3.html

TWO CASE STUDIES

One way to figure out which search engine to go with is to do some testing with the same search on various engines and analyze the results. Let's try a case study. Our assignment: an in-depth story on racial diversity in U.S. newsrooms. We would want to get statistics illustrating both the problem of inequities in newsrooms today and the historical context. We also would want to find out about efforts to diversify newsrooms. And we'd like to get some names of experts who can speak authoritatively about the topic. Our search terms will be "newsroom diversity" (searched as a phrase). For purposes of this illustration, we will analyze only the first 20 results from each search.

Searches of seven popular search engines found programs, studies, and reports on newsroom diversity from the American Society of Newspaper Editors (ASNE), the Associated Press Managing Editors (APME), the Freedom Forum, the Radio–Television News Directors Foundation (RTNDF), the Poynter Institute for Media Studies, the University of Maryland, and the University of North Carolina at Chapel Hill. None of the search engines found all of the above-mentioned sites (at least not in the first 20 results), but some performed better than others. Here are the results:

MetaCrawler: The meta-search engine MetaCrawler produced the best results in this example. MetaCrawler found the sites for everything mentioned above except for the University of North Carolina.

BOX 7.1

Phineas Fiske, an editorial writer for Newsday, *employed search engines to conduct research on electrical deregulation.*

Probably my most challenging assignment as an editorial writer for *Newsday* has been to evaluate plans for restructuring our region's electrical service. Long Island has the highest electric rates in the continental United States, which is a drag on the economy and a frustration for householders. And the utility that serves the region, the Long Island Lighting Co. (LILCO), is reviled by many residents, particularly because it attempted to build a nuclear power plant here. So various political leaders have been trying for a decade to either redress the region's problems or make political hay from them—more often the latter.

The governor of New York, George Pataki, early on after his election committed himself to finding a way to reduce the Island's high electric costs, and commissioned a public agency, the Long Island Power Authority, to do that. The authority came up with a costly proposal to buy out the bulk of LILCO and replace it with a municipal power system.

Into this volatile mix came the evolving story of electric utility competition, which is being touted in much of the country as the clear road to lower electric rates.

So *Newsday's* editorial page has been trying to sort out both the complexities of the power authority's plan and the competing appeal of competition, in the context of a rapidly changing electric industry, in order to decide what is best for Long Island.

The World Wide Web has been an invaluable resource. Using the usual Web search tools (mostly Alta Vista, the search engine I rely on generally) and following Web resources to new ones, I was able to find background information needed to help evaluate the various claims and counterclaims being made. The state utility regulator's site includes all the competition proposals from around New York, handy for comparison. The U.S. Department of Energy has much useful background on the industry, all accessible on the Web. A key order of the Federal Energy Regulatory Agency is also on the Web in its entirety. There are arguments pro and con about electricity competition by involved parties and interest groups, and energy consultants' sites carry rundowns on what other states are doing. I subscribed to a news tracking service, NewsHound, that, in effect, clips current news stories on electricity competition from around the country and alerts me to them daily.

Dealing with a story like this, which is taking place largely at the state level around the country and evolving rapidly as well, there is no one handy authority to turn to for needed information. The Web has provided access to a range of authorities in ways that I can't imagine I'd have had the time to develop otherwise.

Excite: Excite found APME, ASNE, Maryland, Poynter, and RTNDF, but not the Freedom Forum or North Carolina.

AltaVista: AltaVista found North Carolina along with the sites from APME, ASNE, and RTNDF, but not the Freedom Forum, Maryland, or Poynter.

Infoseek: Infoseek found APME, ASNE, Freedom Forum, and RTNDF, but not Maryland, North Carolina, or Poynter.

HotBot: HotBot found APME, ASNE, Maryland, and RTNDF, but not the Freedom Forum, Poynter, or North Carolina.

Lycos: Lycos had the same results as HotBot.

WebCrawler: WebCrawler found only ASNE.

Let's try another case study. This time, instead of doing a basic search of the top 20 results, which measures the accuracy of a search, let's look at the engines according to their comprehensiveness. We will conduct a name search on the author of this book and measure the results. For purposes of this illustration, we will search only on "Christopher Callahan," but for a news story we probably would want also to check on other variations of the name.

In this case, AltaVista and HotBot were by far the most comprehensive.

AltaVista: The AltaVista search found my resumé at the University of Maryland, other mentions in the College of Journalism Web site, an *American Journalism Review* (AJR) article on Internet reporting, an early version of Internet as a Reporting Tool Web site at Harvard University, a Finnish site that refers to the Harvard site, numerous Capital News Service citations, an article from a Maryland alumni magazine, several campus newspaper articles, citations from journalism classes at the University of Southern California and Louisiana State University, a resumé that lists me as a reference, and even results from some local 10K road races.

HotBot: HotBot found sites that AltaVista did not, including an article from the *National Association of Black Journalist's Journal*, several college guides, several scholastic journalism guides, a Danish reference to the Harvard site, a citation on a New Zealand commercial Web site, and a quote from a campus newspaper at the University of Missouri. But it did not find some of what AltaVista came up with, including the resumé, alumni magazine, campus dailies, and some of the running results.

Excite: Excite found the *AJR* article, the Capital News Service information, the Harvard site, and one of the road race results. It also found a reference not picked up by the other search engines from a Society of Professional Journalists page.

MetaCrawler: MetaCrawler found the resumé, the *AJR* article, the Harvard site and Finnish link to that site, and the Capital News Service references.

Infoseek: Infoseek came up with the resumé, the Harvard site, the *AJR* article, the Capital News Service page, and one of the road races.

WebCrawler: WebCrawler found only the *AJR* article and Harvard site.

Lycos: Lycos found only the Harvard site.

HOW MANY SEARCHES?

How many searches should you conduct on how many different search engines? There is no easy answer, but remember that you are using the Internet in part to *save* yourself reporting time. It is easy to get so caught up in trying to find the information on various search engines that you wind up wasting too much time. I recommend that, for deadline reporting, first think about the best search terms and then conduct that search on one or two search engines, taking advantage of the specific search commands for those engines. After that there are diminishing returns, as you see from the previous examples.

Now that we have some search strategies to go with our knowledge of the Web and our specific Web sites, let's put it all together in developing an electronic beat system.

▶ 8

Building an Electronic Beat

The first few hours and days on a new beat, or in a new newsroom, are spent quickly getting up to speed on the issues and players to be covered. The first stop is getting briefed by veteran editors, reporters and, when possible, the person whose beat you are taking over. Next is thumbing through recent clips. Then, time permitting, you might go out and introduce yourself to new sources, perhaps collecting background information, documents, and directories along the way. The idea is to familiarize yourself quickly with the territory and gather sources and resources that can be accessed quickly on deadline. And, ideally, you will have a chance to do all of this *before* you have to begin filing daily stories.

We should take this same approach in creating an Internet beat system—gathering, organizing, and familiarizing ourselves with potentially useful sources of information while *not* on deadline. With an electronic beat system already in place, we then can jump on the Internet with confidence to access information quickly and effectively on deadline.

We will find beat-specific Internet sites by tapping into the search skills from the previous chapter in addition to the source lists of Chapters 4, 5, and 6. Each site should be examined to find out where the useful information is located. And we will organize these beat sites by using the bookmarks learned in Chapter 2 (p. 14) so these sources can be quickly accessed under deadline pressure.

TYPES OF BEATS

All beats can be broken down into three basic categories—geographic-based beats (the Washington County reporter), issue-oriented beats (the environmental reporter), and beats that cover institutions (the City Hall reporter).

All reporters fall into one of those three categories, even general assignment reporters (the circulation area that their publications cover is a geographic beat). Let's look at how we can find and organize Internet sources for each of these three beat types.

THE GEOGRAPHIC BEAT

Desktop Reporting Tools. The basic reporting tools discussed in Chapter 4—Web phone directories and crisscross directories, mapping programs, expert source databases, the Census Bureau Statistical Abstract, the customizable Freedom of Information Act and state public records law templates, and the state open meeting and public records law—all should be bookmarked. These tools will be the same whether the beat is geographic, issue-, or institution-based.

Daily News. Use *AJR* NewsLink (p. 52, www.ajr.org) or NewsCentral (p. 52, www.all-links.com/newscentral) to find the appropriate local and regional daily newspapers. Then check via AP's The Wire (p. 52, wire.ap.org) to find which papers carry the local and national wire services on the Web and bookmark those sites. You also may want to include major national publications such as the *New York Times* for potential story ideas that can be localized.

Demographic Data. Bookmark not only the main Census Bureau Web page (p. 34, www.census.gov) but click down and bookmark the census pages for new press releases and customizable census databases for your town or county. Also locate your state data center via the Census Bureau, explore that site, and bookmark the useful sections. Demographic data is especially important if a reporter is new to the area.

State Government. Locate your state's main Web site via GlobalComputing (p. 49, www.globalcomputing.com/states.html) and bookmark it. You also may want to find and bookmark some key pages, such as an employees' directory and the state government manual.

State Legislature. Bookmark the state Legislature home page and the pages of your local state lawmakers.

Local Government. Find your town, city and/or county government either through the state Web site or via one of the search engines or directories discussed in the previous chapter. Spend some time learning what is available on the sites. Bookmark the home page plus useful pages inside.

Schools. Using a Web directory or search engine, locate and bookmark Web sites for both the local school systems and area colleges and universities.

Major Employers. Find, evaluate, and bookmark the company We. for each of the major employers and public utilities in your covera area by using the methods in Chapter 7. Then go to the Securities and Exchange Commission, the Occupational Safety and Health Administration, and FECInfo sites (listed in Chapter 5) and bookmark the data pages for those companies.

Special Interest Groups. Employ search engines to find the local special interest groups in your area, including lobbying groups, nonprofit organizations and associations, unions, business groups, community and civic organizations, and churches. Then, traveling down from the main state Web page, find and bookmark the secretary of state's page on corporate and nonprofit filings.

Local Politics. Using either the Republican (www.rnc.org) and Democratic (www.dem.org) national Web sites (p. 45) or search engines, find and save the locations for the state parties, county parties, and local politicians. This is useful not only to access information for stories, but to monitor how politicians and political parties are communicating with their constituencies and what they are saying.

Courts. Check through the state government home page or via LegalOnline (p. 47, www.legalonline.com) to search for state appellate courts online. Then bookmark the appropriate U.S. Circuit Court, the U.S. Supreme Court, and other legal resources from Chapter 5 (p. 47).

Federal Register. Go to the Federal Register (p. 38) and bookmark it to conduct regular searches for federal government actions and proposals affecting the town, city, or county you are covering.

Search Engines. Bookmark your favorite search engines for quick access.

THE ISSUE BEAT

The Web sites for desktop reporting tools, daily news, and search engines are the same as those listed previously for the locale-based beat. But there are some substantial differences.

State Government. In addition to the general state government Web page, surf down to locate and analyze the state agencies that regulate your issue. Bookmark not only the main agency page but also inside pages that may be particularly valuable in your reporting.

State Legislature. Bookmark the main state Legislature page and committees dealing with your subject area.

Chapter 8

BOX 8.1

Frank Sweeney explains how the Internet helped the San Jose Mercury News *cover devastating California floods.*

Our coverage of the floods of 1997 had a high-tech edge.

Some reporters made extensive use of the National Weather Service's home page from Monterey (www.nws.mbay.net), in particular its link to the river and rainfall page, where there are links to river flow reporting stations.

We could see, hour by hour, how high the water was rising on the big rivers of the Central Valley, and how much was flowing into and out of the major reservoirs. For some rivers, there were graphs showing the rise and fall of the water compared to the flood-stage level.

The California Data Exchange Center home page (cyclone.water.ca.gov) has links to hundreds of gauges and sensors that measure river flow, rainfall, and temperatures. This page even offered aerial photos of flooded areas and maps of levee breaks.

And late in the game, I found the Winter Storm and Flood Page (www.oes.ca.gov:8001/html/flood.html), which offers a wealth of information. These pages, set up for flood-control and water managers, aren't necessarily user-friendly. They take a little getting used to. The National Weather Service page is a lot easier to decipher.

Local Government. Save the main page and the local government agencies that affect your issue.

Special Interest Groups. Find the local, state, and national special interest groups that are players on your issue beat, including lobbying groups, business associations, unions, and other organizations.

Federal Agencies. Find the federal agencies dealing with your issue, surf those sites, and bookmark the main pages and useful inside pages.

Specialty Publications. Employing either search engines or MediaFinder (p. 56, www.mediafinder.com), locate and bookmark the specialty newsletters and magazines that follow your issue.

Journalism Organizations. Check Chapter 12 to see if there are any journalism organizations that specialize in your beat area. These can provide various resources and indicate other good sources.

BOX 8.2

Heather Newman of the Detroit Free Press *tapped the power of the Internet for an in-depth look at standardized tests for Michigan elementary schools.*

We did a major project early in 1998 looking at our state standardized tests for elementary schools in Michigan. The project never would have been possible without computers, and would not have been as complete or as timely without the Internet. The thrust of our project was this: Educators had been telling us that school test scores could be dramatically affected by factors outside of schools' control, such as poverty or the education of the parents. Yet standardized tests in Michigan are used for everything from custody battles to real estate listings, and the state accreditation formula, which affects how schools are funded, depends almost entirely on one set of tests: the Michigan Educational Assessment Program, or MEAP scores.

We set out to determine what, if any, effect factors outside of districts' control had on test scores and whether those scores were being used wisely. It was a six-month project, scheduled between daily and shorter efforts. We started by sending out a request to ProfNet (profnet@profnet.com) for experts who could help us, and searching their expert database (www.profnet.com) to see whether we could turn up any names there. We got more than three dozen responses, all educational statisticians who could help us structure our analysis.

Next, we turned to the Net for Web sites that had information about standardized testings, which eventually turned into a sidebar for the main piece. This directed us toward more experts we could consult and additional factors we could consider when analyzing the tests. We also used Lexis–Nexis to hunt for packages written by other newspapers and magazines that might mirror what we were trying to do.

Once we had a list of factors that might affect test scores, given to us by our experts and our research, we set out to find that data on a district or school level for Michigan. All the data the state education office kept, including many of the factors we needed, was on their Web site in searchable or downloadable form. We also discovered, through the Web, two CD-ROMs produced by the U.S. Department of Education and the National Center for Education Statistics (the School District Data Book [SDDB] and the Common Core of Data), which included yet more information about districts and schools across the state. We ordered both these discs (one is free; the other costs $15). When technical problems arose with the SDDB, we contacted the person who handled tech support for the program via E-mail, and he E-mailed the solutions back to us and attached some files we needed to his correspondence.

We combined all these databases into one huge data set that included hundreds of bits of information on each of Michigan's 500-plus school districts.

(Continued)

BOX 8.2 *Continued*

Then we set about doing our analysis, based on the advice we had gotten from our experts and some standard statistics techniques. We found that, in urban and surburban areas, factors beyond a district's control accounted for the majority of differences between districts' scores, which meant that what was happening inside the classroom had less effect than what was happening at home. We E-mailed the results of our study and the supporting comput-

er files to a few statisticians, who reviewed our work for us to make sure we had dotted our *i*'s and crossed our *t*'s.

We conducted many of our interviews via E-mail, and set up quite a few of the ones we conducted in person using E-mail messages. Without the Internet, the project would not have had nearly the depth it did, nor would it have been as successful.

Beat Organizers. Some Internet-savvy journalists have shared their own electronic beat systems with fellow reporters on the Web. Phineas Fiske of *Newsday* has put together an impressive collection of sites for editorial writers at

www.ncew.org

Shawn McIntosh of the *Dallas Morning News* also has a site for issue-oriented beat reporters at

www.reporter.org/beat

You undoubtedly will find Web resources on these pages that you have yet to come across. But I strongly recommend that you look at these reporter sites only *after* you have done the searches on your own. The power of creating a beat-oriented list of resources is that it is tailored specifically to you and your publication. That cannot be reproduced en masse.

THE INSTITUTION BEAT

The institution-based beat is analogous to the issue beat. The same categories can be applied.

So far in this book we have looked at the World Wide Web portion of the Internet. In the next three chapters, we will look at some other Internet tools that can help reporters and editors, beginning with electronic mail.

▶ 9

Electronic Mail

Bill Loving, the computer-assisted reporting editor at the Minneapolis *Star Tribune*, says electronic mail is "replacing the fax as the communication tool of choice." He's right. E-mail is faster than faxes, usually arriving in a matter of moments, while faxes often get caught up on busy phone lines, jammed and backed-up fax machines, or machines out of paper. E-mail is cheaper than faxes, costing only the monthly Internet connection fees in contrast to the long-distance telephone charges and paper for fax machines. E-mail is more reliable than faxes, landing directly in a person's electronic mail system instead of arriving on a fax machine likely shared by an entire office. And E-mail holds more potential as an innovative reporting tool.

E-MAIL AS A REPORTING TOOL

Routine Deadline Reporting Questions. If you need to find out a relatively simple piece of information from a source, such as getting a single fact confirmed, an E-mail can help circumvent those dreaded late afternoon games of phone tag that turn reporters prematurely gray. E-mail often will get returned more quickly than the phone message because it is faster and easier for the source. You would not want to conduct in-depth interviews via E-mail, but for the perfunctory question, it can be a valuable time-saver.

Contacting Hard-to-Reach Sources. Sometimes E-mail is the best, or perhaps only way, to contact a source. Phineas Fiske, an editorial writer at *Newsday*, tells the story of his efforts to track down a former state official who was traveling in Russia and could not be reached. Fiske, knowing the former official traveled with a laptop computer, sent a message to his E-mail address. The source responded within hours.

Contacting Reluctant Sources. We all have experienced the source who is integral to the story, but ducks us at every turn and refuses to return phone messages. Or perhaps you cannot even get past roadblocks set up by overprotective secretaries or paranoid public relations officers. E-mail is another way to make direct contact, allowing you to make your case about why the source should agree to an interview. And, unlike traditional mail and even phone messages, E-mail usually goes directly to the person, not through a secretary, assistant, or flak.

Contacting Web Masters. By now you are probably familiar with the E-mail addresses for "web masters"—the techies who run the Web sites—located at the bottom of most home pages. Neill A. Borowski, director of computer-assisted reporting and analysis at the *Philadelphia Inquirer,* suggests writing to Web masters when looking for data that is not available on the Web pages, but may exist somewhere within the agency that runs the Web site. Borowski E-mailed the Web master of the New Jersey State Data Center requesting housing data from the 1970 and 1980 census for particular New Jersey towns. He received the data within a day.

Contacting Multiple Sources Quickly. E-mail also is a fast and efficient way to contact numerous sources on the same subject. For instance, in the preparation of this book, I wanted to contact journalists who I thought were some of the best in Internet reporting and ask them to contribute a piece. It would have taken me days to reach each journalist by telephone, but the E-mail connections took just a few moments.

Keeping in Touch with Sources. E-mail also is a good way to keep in contact with sources. After his series on toxins in fertilizer (p. 4), Duff Wilson of the *Seattle Times* sent the story and follow-ups to more than 50 sources, asking for their comments. He reported getting leads on several follow-up stories from the E-mail contacts.

Exchanging Ideas with Colleagues. Among the wonderful things about journalism are the professional bonds and friendships formed among colleagues. Some of my best friends—and people I respect most professionally—are the journalists I worked with at my college newspaper and my first jobs out of school. But, of course, most of those folks are now scattered across the country. E-mail provides a way to stay connected with those people and to exchange ideas and concerns about stories and other journalism issues. It can be quite helpful to have a trusted colleague read a draft of a big enterprise package before sending it off to your editor. The more input you have on a piece of journalism from colleagues whom you trust and respect, the better the finished product will be.

Connection to Readers. Some publications are beginning to include reporters' E-mail addresses at the end of stories so that readers can contact them directly. This has limited use. Certainly hearing reader feedback to stories is important, but such unsolicited comments often come from the extreme ends of a given issue. Furthermore, people connected to E-mail still do not represent a socioeconomic cross section of the country.

Over the Transom Sources. E-mail also provides another outlet for new sources to provide tips, but again caution should be exercised. Never assume that people who contact you via E-mail are actually who they say they are. Always check it out.

Electronic Releases and Updates. Some agencies, corporations, and special interest groups are beginning to send out regular alerts and press releases to interested reporters via E-mail instead of fax (see p. 81).

DECODING E-MAIL ADDRESSES

There are several ways to find E-mail addresses. The best for journalists (because it is the fastest) is making an educated guess, in much the same way we guessed at Web addresses in Chapter 7. But in order to make a good guess, we need to decipher E-mail addresses.

Computer Host Addresses. E-mail addresses have two main parts, divided by an "at" sign (@). The part after the @ symbol is the address of the computer that is hosting the E-mail user. These host addresses are similar to the home page addresses of Web pages. They have two or more parts separated by dots. Reading from right to left, the parts of the host computer address go from the most general to the most specific. The section furthest to the right uses the same three-letter suffixes as we saw in the Web addresses in Chapter 3 (.com = commercial sites,.gov = government sites,.edu = education sites, and so on). Let's use an example. My friend Kevin Galvin works for the Associated Press. His E-mail address at work is

kgalvin@ap.org

In this case, ap.org is the computer address. Reading from right to left, "org" stands for a nonprofit organization. Next comes an abbreviation for the institution of the host computer, in this case "ap" for Associated Press. From this analysis we can deduce that AP employees have E-mail addresses that end "@ap.org". All E-mail addresses can be analyzed in the same way.

Let's look at another example. My friend Mitch Zuckoff works at the *Boston Globe.* His E-mail address is zuckof@nws.globe.com

The ".com" means it is a commercial site. "Globe" is an abbreviation for the host computer, in this case the *Boston Globe*. And "nws" stands for a section or department within the main institution, in this case the news department of the *Globe*. From this we can conclude that news employees at the *Boston Globe* have E-mail addresses that end with "@nws.globe.com". We also can guess that *Globe* employees who are not part of the news department probably have different E-mail addresses (@???.globe.com).

User Identifications. Now let's tackle the first part of the E-mail address, known as the user ID. Because E-mail systems are developed in large part so people within the same organization can communicate easily with each other, computer system designers usually create user-ID systems that are uniform. This avoids the problem of having to memorize or look up E-mail addresses each time you want to send an electronic message. Common user-ID systems include the first and last name, the last name then the first name, the first initial of the first name and the full last name, the last name then the first initial of the first name, just the last name, and just a specified number of letters from the last name. Looking at our examples, we can tell from Kevin Galvin's address (kgalvin) that the AP user-ID system is the first initial of the first name and the full last name. That means we now know the precise E-mail for virtually everyone who works at the *Associated Press*. For our other example, it appears the *Globe* uses a system of the first six letters of the user's last name (zuckof).

FINDING E-MAIL ADDRESSES

Guessing. Now that we know how to analyze electronic mail system addresses, we can guess at the E-mail addresses of sources once we have the address for at least one other person in that organization. This can be a powerful tool in your reporting. For instance, most public relations officers would give you their E-mail addresses, but might be reluctant to hand out the addresses of the agency head or other potential news sources in the organization. Armed only with the PR officer's E-mail address, you probably can deduce the addresses for everyone else there.

Institutional Directories. What if you do not have any E-mail addresses at an institution? Then you should find the institution's Web site and search for a directory of addresses.

General E-Mail Directories. What if the institution does not have an E-mail directory or if the person you are looking for is not part of a large institution? In those cases, go to one of a variety of electronic mail search engines. The search engines are similar to the programs that look for Web sites discussed in Chapter 7. They are found on both the telephone directories discussed in Chapter 4 and on the major search engines.

Fingering an E-Mail Address. This is a method of obtaining more information about the person behind the E-mail, such as his or her address and institutional affiliation. Many addresses, however, are not included, and remember that it is relatively easy to fake an E-mail identity. To try a finger program, go to:

www.cs.indiana.edu:800/finger/gateway

NEWSROOM POLICIES ON E-MAIL COMMUNICATION

The Associated Press has some specific guidelines for the use of E-mail in reporting. They include:

- Represent the organization. An E-mail with a reporter's affiliation attached is similar to that reporter appearing at a public meeting or writing a letter on company letterhead.
- Avoid political activity. "AP has long-standing rules against News employees participating in political activities or taking sides on matters of public debate," the policy states. "These rules apply to electronic communication as well."
- Follow the etiquette of E-mail (such as not typing in all capital letters, which can be perceived by recipients as *shouting* electronically).
- Check all E-mail sources of information. Remember that E-mail addresses can be faked.

PROFNET

We talked about the ProfNet database of expert sources back in Chapter 4, but ProfNet is best known to reporters as an E-mail system for finding expert sources. ProfNet will take a reporter's E-mail request for a particular type of expert source and distribute it to public relations offices in about 2,000 institutions worldwide, including 760 universities, 500 corporations, 380 PR firms, 300 nonprofit organizations and government agencies, and 100 think tanks, scientific associations, and labs. Reporter requests are sent out three times a day (10:30 A.M., 1:30 P.M., and 4 P.M. Eastern time) to the 4,300 participating public relations officials. It is the same idea as calling your local university for an expert source, but, instead of making one phone call, you are making 2,000 simultaneously.

ProfNet has grown dramatically since it was started by Daniel Forbush at the State University of New York at Stony Brook in the early 1990s. It is now run by PR NewsWire and handles 60 to 80 reporter requests a day.

To use ProfNet, send an E-mail query to profnet@profnet.com or use the E-mail form available from the ProfNet home page (www.profnet.com) (see Figure 9.1). ProfNet can also be contacted directly at:

www.prnewswire.com/cgi-bin/profnet/profsearch.pl

Reporters also can phone in ProfNet requests (1-800-PROFNET) or fax (516-689-1425).

Some keys to a ProfNet search include:

Deadlines. ProfNet is designed for enterprise stories, not spot news coverage. Also, make sure to include a deadline in your message (the "deadline" should be when you need to hear from the source, not when the story is actually due to your editor).

Specificity. You are not looking for dozens of potential sources, you are seeking the small handful of truly expert sources for your story. The best ProfNet requests are the ones that have a great deal of specificity.

Audience. Think about what types of institutions should receive your request. If you want your request to go only to universities and think tanks, for instance, make that clear in your query.

Identification. Make it clear whom you represent and describe your news organization in terms of type of publication, audience, and circulation.

Response. Specify how you want to be contacted (E-mail, phone, or fax).

Confidentiality. ProfNet searches are supposed to be confidential, but if you are working on a particularly sensitive story be sure to write your query in a way that does not tip off the story. You also can cloak your identity (but if you are sitting on the next Watergate, probably best to skip ProfNet altogether).

Verification. And, of course, once you have gotten the names and numbers of some sources, do not just assume they are truly expert on your topic. Check them out by asking the PR officials to provide the potential sources' credentials on the subject at hand. Or better yet, find the experts on the Web and check out their background yourself. Just because you found the sources through a ProfNet query, that does not make the sources any better (or worse) on their face than if you had called the university, nonprofit, or think tank.

Welcome to ──

ProfNet

The Shortest Distance Between A Journalist And A Source

Good sources are hard to find. That's why we created ProfNet, a collaborative of 4,000 public relations professionals linked by Internet to give journalists and authors convenient access to expert sources.

For Reporters

For News & Information Officers

We're a direct link to 4,300 news and information officers at colleges and universities, corporations, think tanks, national labs, medical centers, non-profits, and PR agencies.

We're a central collection-and-distribution point for reporters' queries. Assisting on hundreds of media projects weekly, we plug you into a more productive approach to media relations.

Navigating ProfNet

FIGURE 9.1   Copyright ProfNet, Inc. Used by permission.

The only difference—and it's a big one—is that you have widened your search enormously. As the *Washington Post*'s Boyce Rensberger said about ProfNet: "You can catch sources that you never would have thought to go after. It's the difference between fishing with a hook and fishing with a net."

ELECTRONIC PRESS RELEASES AND NEWS ALERTS

More government agencies, companies, and special interest groups are making press releases and other news alerts available via E-mail. The automated systems are similar to the mailing lists described in the next chapter. Reporters electronically subscribe to a particular list, and they automatically receive that organization's releases. The E-mail press release has several advantages over the traditional fax. It is faster, it is more reliable (E-mail comes directly to the recipient's account, while faxes are usually shared by an entire newsroom or section of the newsroom and can get lost), and it is cheaper (it saves on fax paper).

Bill Dedman, the Pulitzer prize-winning reporter of the *Atlanta Constitution,* now in Chicago writing for the *New York Times,* has done extensive research on the proliferation of E-mail news alerts. The information in Box 9.1 that follows is excerpted from his Web site. The full site is available at:

home.att.net/~bdedman/alert.html

BOX 9.1

U.S. Bureau of the Census

> www.census.gov/mp/www/
> subscribe.html

The Census Bureau has several services, including announcements of upcoming data releases. You can subscribe to any of four alerts: Monthly Product Announcement and Daily List (biweekly accumulations of materials published in the past period), the Census I-Net Bulletin (biweekly suggestions of stories and new data sources), Census and You (monthly feature ideas, often tied to holidays), and Press Releases (periodic, often giving you the jump on upcoming data releases and reports). This last is the best, because it gives you a chance to do some reporting on the data, or your own analysis, before the embargo date.

U.S. Consumer Product Safety Commission

> www.cpsc.gov

You can automatically get product recall notices from the Consumer Product Safety Commission. Send an E-mail to listproc@cpsc.gov with the text, "Subscribe CPSCINFO-L."

U.S. Department of Agriculture

> usda.mannlib.cornell.edu/usda/
> emailinfo.html

Everything from chickens to cranberries. The Ag Department has 70 reports, including information on imports, exports, prices, chemicals, milk, et al.

U.S. Department of Education

> www.ed.gov/MailingLists

The most recent news from the Education Department.

U.S. Federal Aviation Administration

> www.faa.gov/apa/pr/
> subscribe.cfm

FAA press releases are sent via E-mail several times a month.

U.S. Federal Communications Commission

> www.fcc.gov/Daily_Releases/
> Daily_Digest/1998/ddhome.html

The FCC Daily Digest provides a synopsis of commission orders, news releases, speeches, and titles of public notices. The Digest is published every business afternoon.

U.S. Federal Emergency Management Agency

> www.fema.gov/fema/listsrv.htm

FEMA has three lists. The "news" list distributes news releases, the "sitrep" list provides subscribers with abridged major disaster situation reports, and the "presidential" list is limited to declarations of major disasters.

U.S. General Accounting Office

> www.gao.gov/cgi-bin/subday.pl

A lot of journalists use this one. The GAO Daybook is a daily update on reports, documents, and testimony. It comes in two forms: an announcement by title and number of pages; and, a few days later, with a URL to the GAO site. The GAO has an order form on the site.

BOX 9.1 *Continued*

U.S. Nuclear Regulatory Commission

www.nrc.gov/NRC/NEWS/
elecinfo.html#nrclists

The NRC has several lists, generating a few messages each a week.

White House press releases

www.whitehouse.gov

To subscribe to White House press releases, send an E-mail to Publications@Pub.Pub.WhiteHouse.gov with the subject line "hello."

Legal Information Institute

www.law.cornell.edu/focus/
bulletins.html

U.S. Supreme Court opinions are distributed, in syllabus form, by Cornell University's Legal Information Institute within hours of their release. This site also has the New York Court of Appeals. Willamette University College of Law runs a similar service, also with the Ninth Circuit Court of Appeals decisions

www.willamette.edu/law/wlo/

The Office of Justice Programs

www.ncjrs.org/ojjdp/html/
jjust.html

The U.S. Department of Justice operates a list on juvenile justice issues. It provides backgrounders and notices on youth crime and violence.

Securities and Exchange Commission (SEC)

Filings by public companies to the U.S. Securities and Exchange Commission are offered by several companies. These companies distribute documents from the SEC's EDGAR service, an acronym for Electronic Data Gathering and Retrieval. All public companies are required to file most of their SEC forms electronically. (The official EDGAR is at www.sec.gov/edgarhp.htm) Two examples are WhoWhere? Inc. (www.whowhere.com/Edgar/index.html) and FreeEDGAR Watchlist (www.freeedgar.com). You can set it up either to send you E-mail when any new forms, or certain types of forms, such as quarterly reports, come in from companies you specify. A variety of services, such as searches by an executive's name, are offered for a fee by EDGAR Online, from Cybernet Data Systems, Inc.

U.S. Centers for Disease Control

www.cdc.gov/subscribe.html

The CDC offers 17 lists, on infectious diseases, HIV/AIDS, morbidity and mortality, minority health, and national health surveys. Also, the CDC National AIDS Clearinghouse has a list at:

www.cdcnac.org/listhelp.html

U.S. Food and Drug Administration

www.fda.gov

FDA sends out safety alerts, public health advisories, and other FDA safety notices. To subscribe, send mail to fdalists@www.fda.gov with the text, "subscribe dev-alert."

National Science Foundation

www.nsf.gov/home/cns/
start.htm

NSF offers an E-mail alert of all new publications, or only those matching

(Continued)

BOX 9.1 *Continued*

your interests, or will make a custom Web page for you.

EurekAlert!

www.eurekalert.org

EurekAlert! is produced by the American Association for the Advancement of Science (AAAS). It offers two daily E-mail notices for reporters and editors only. One is a list of scientific research papers, but you have to agree to honor the embargo and be reviewed for the privilege. The other is a daily news headlines listing. All news comes from universities and scientific organizations that pay fees to EurekAlert!

U.S. Environmental Protection Agency

www.epa.gov/epahome/
listserv.htm

EPA has nearly 40 alerts, covering topics from endangered species to international issues to U.S. regional information. EPA also has an E-mail tip of the week; to subscribe, send mail to tnielsen@ercweb.com with the word "subscribe" as the subject of the message. Include a complete name, compa-

ny, E-mail address, and U.S. mail address in the body of the message.

Environmental News Network

www.enn.com/news/
enewswire-signup.htm

ENN's Newswire is a daily digest of environmental news.

Environmental TipSheet

www.sej.org

TipSheet is a biweekly environmental list of story ideas from the Society of Environmental Journalists, the Radio and Television News Directors Foundation, and the Environmental Health Center. To subscribe, send an E-mail to majordomo@sej.org with the text, "subscribe sejtipsheet yourfirstname yourlastname yourmail."

Center for Responsive Politics

www.crp.org

Political junkies will appreciate the alerts from the Center for Responsive Politics, a nonprofit that monitors campaign contributions.

E-MAIL AS NEWS

A growing area of electronic mail for journalists is the idea of E-mail as public documents. State statutes and case law vary on this question, but it can be a treasure trove of news stories for investigative reporters. Look at the public records law in your state (p. 32) to find out whether e-mail transmissions by public officials are considered open records.

► 10

Mailing Lists: E-Mail Discussion Groups

The previous chapter discussed how to use electronic mail on a one-to-one basis and how to receive news releases and alerts. But the Internet also allows users to quickly send E-mail to special-interest groups. There are more than 100,000 of these "mailing lists," discussion groups on specific topics that allow a user to send a single message to one site and have that message distributed automatically and simultaneously to everyone who has subscribed to that particular list. Users then can respond to the entire membership of the list simply by responding to the list address. Subject areas range from everything from botany to Bob Dylan. Most mailing lists are "open," or "public," meaning anyone can subscribe. Some are "closed," or "private," which means you have to obtain permission from the list manager to subscribe. Most lists are unmoderated, but some have moderators who filter the content that goes out. Nearly all the lists are free.

These mailing lists, or discussion groups, are sometimes referred to generically as "listservs." But Listserv is actually the corporate name for just one type of mailing list, and Listserv lists make up only a portion of all Internet mailing lists. Listproc and Majordomo are two other popular mailing list services. We will learn about how to use all of these mailing lists later in this chapter, but first let's explore some of the journalistic reasons why we want to try these discussion groups.

JOURNALISTIC USES OF MAILING LISTS

Search for Expert Sources. Reporters can send E-mail to a mailing list in search of expert sources on a particular story. There are electronic discussion groups on virtually every topic, from the environment and higher education to crime and politics.

Searching for "Regular People" Sources. Reporters also can send E-mail to a mailing list in search of "regular people" to help put a face on a feature or enterprise story. Let's say you are writing a feature story on the trend in home beer brewing. You could subscribe to one of the home brewers' listservs (BEER-L or HOMEBREW) and send a query asking for home brewers in your area. It is amazing how specific some of these lists can get. For instance, not only are there dozens of discussion groups for jazz aficionados, but there is one devoted exclusively to an ongoing dialogue on the music of the late jazz trumpeter Miles Davis. My favorite on the obscurity scale is the "Star Trek from a Jewish Cultural Religious Perspective" discussion group. But treat the responses with the same caution as an unsolicited E-mail from an unknown source. You need to verify that the potential sources are indeed who they claim to be.

Listening In. Good reporters eavesdrop. We listen to conversations among schoolteachers before the school board meeting. We perk up as lawyers chat at the courthouse. We catch snippets of discussions among cops at the station house. We listen to neighbors complaining at the grocery store, dry cleaners, and neighborhood bar. And that's a good thing. That is in part how we find new stories on our beats.

Discussion groups are another way to "listen in" on conversations. Reporters can subscribe to lists in their topic area and "listen" to the conversations by monitoring the E-mail exchanges (this is referred to as "lurking" in Internet parlance).

Professional Development. There are dozens of journalism-related mailing lists with ongoing discussions on everything from computer-assisted reporting to newsroom ethics. Joining one or more of the groups can expose you to new reporting techniques, story ideas, upcoming contests or programs, or, perhaps just let you vent about a recent ethical dilemma or newsroom frustration.

WARNINGS

Before you sign up for any mailing lists, a few warnings:

Weed through the Garbage. Like everything else on the Internet, the overwhelming majority of things you will find on mailing lists are journalistically worthless. Discussion groups are renowned for endless chitchat, mindless bickering, off-topic discussions, people who like to "hear" themselves talk, and those who clearly have way too much time on their hands. My favorite discussion group "thread" (Internet jargon for multiple messages on the same topic) is a discussion of how the discussion

---

BOX 10.1

Mark Schleifstein of the New Orleans Times Picayune *describes how his use of Internet discussion groups helped him report a series on oceans that won the 1997 Pulitzer prize for Public Service Reporting.*

In December 1994, I wrote a simple paragraph that set in motion the biggest reporting project I've ever been involved with.

My editors had come to me and asked for ideas about projects for the coming year. I glanced through my list of story ideas in my computer and found this note at the very bottom: "The fisheries beat no longer exists. It's covered by a variety of people when a story comes up, but no one spends all their time messing around with it anymore."

The note had been sent to me by an editor several years ago when I asked whether the suburban reporter who had been covering fisheries could pick up a story I was too busy for. I thought about that note, and about my own reporting on habitat-related issues involving Louisiana's wetlands, and wrote the following: "Seafood: We need to do a major take-out on how the rapidly declining stocks of a variety of seafood species, ranging from redfish to shrimp to sea trout, are affecting the state. This is a huge story that we've covered poorly on a daily basis, inasmuch as seafood is the third or fourth largest industry in the state. I see this as a bells-and-whistles project."

I sent the note to my editor and forgot about it.

Two weeks later, he was back at my desk. "Well, you're the project."

The editors had met and decided to team me with three people: John Mc-

Quaid, our Washington correspondent, who has quite a bit of experience covering environmental issues, both in Congress and during a two-year stint as our Central American correspondent; Bob Marshall, our nationally respected outdoors writer, who also writes regularly for *Field and Stream* magazine; and photographer Ted Jackson, whose expertise is capturing both complicated people stories and wildlife stories on film.

Trying to keep track of what we were doing—and keep us on track—was Political Editor Tim Morris.

There was only one problem: Was there really a story in fish? The four of us were told to find out—fast.

We called a number of scientists, fisheries experts, biologists, wetlands experts, and politicians. Ironically, they all gave us similar answers.

"Problem? There's no problem. Management is working. We learned our lesson in the Gulf of Mexico from the collapse of commercial fisheries in New England and Alaska. In 20 years, we'll still have enough fish to keep both commercial fishers and recreational anglers happy."

But when we then asked, "What about wetlands loss? What happens if Louisiana continues to lose 25 square miles of wetlands a year?" the answers changed.

"Oh, wetlands loss. Well, if nothing's done, in 20 years there won't be any commercial amounts of fish in the Gulf."

(Continued)

BOX 10.1 *Continued*

We knew we had a story.

Now, all we had to do was learn everything we could about fish as fast as we could.

As it turned out, we all leaned on the Internet to speed up that process.

Producing our series was a lesson in the value of E-mail as a source of sources, both people and documents. For me, using the Net is an intuitive process. I tend to treat Web sites and E-mail the same way I treat the remote control for my television: I switch around a lot until I find something that interests me, and then settle down to study.

I figured one of the places to start our search for information was to find listservs that dealt with fisheries issues.

When we began our project, America Online had its own searchable list of listservs, so I started there, although today there are several Internet sites that serve the same purpose. I typed in the word *Fisheries* and checked what turned up, and then used other words, like *ocean* and *habitat* and *wetland,* to expand my choices. Several listservs seemed to cover subjects dealing with fisheries. Here are some examples:

AQUA-L is a list for aquaculture businessmen and scientists. I met Bob Rosenberry, the publisher of *Shrimp News International,* on this list. His publication, aimed at shrimp farmers worldwide, provided me with quite a few leads to track down the spread of Taura, a virus that kills farmed shrimp in the United States and around the world.

BENTHOS is devoted to organisms that live on the bottom of the sea. This list proved useful in my research on the effects of the Dead Zone on the

bottom of the Gulf of Mexico. The Dead Zone, an area of water that some years is 7,000 square miles in size and stretches from the Mississippi River's mouth to the Texas border, is very low in oxygen content. Fish and shrimp avoid the area, much to the chagrin of fishers, and the benthos—everything from starfish to clams to worms, are killed.

FISHFOLK is a discussion of social science and fisheries, used by sociologists, anthropologists, and economists. John used this list to gather quite a bit of information about the effects of a system called "individual transferable quotas" that was being considered as a tool for limiting the number of fishers on both the East and West coasts. John also met his wife—an anthropologist who worked at Woods Hole Oceanographic Institute—through the list (see p. 102).

INFOTERRA is an environmentalist-oriented worldwide list that proved quite useful over the past year in our coverage of issues involving gold mining in Indonesia by Freeport-McMoRan, a Fortune 500 company based in New Orleans. We were able to track rumors involving the Bre-X gold mine scam on this list, because it is used by quite a few NGOs (nongovernmental organizations) dealing with indigenous peoples.

John and I started signing up for a number of the lists.

I already was a member of SEJ-L, the Society of Environmental Journalists listserv, as well as CARR-L and NICAR-L, all of which proved useful during the project.

After we signed up for several lists, we sat back and *lurked,* a term describing a subscriber who receives mes-

BOX 10.1 *Continued*

sages, but doesn't participate in the discussion.

We soon learned that each of these lists had different purposes and different members. Some had their own internal political battles going on. Some were in the midst of flame wars. Others were moderated. With the fish lists, we soon found ourselves inundated with information.

On FISHFOLK, for instance, sociologists and biologists and icthyologists were discussing the effects of overfishing on specific fisheries.

An official with the Congressional Research Service was posting a weekly summary of fisheries news he gathered for congressional leaders. That alone was worth the price of admission, as it provided us with valuable leads on everything from the shooting war that broke out between Spain and Canada over fishing rights for turbot, a type of halibut found off the coast of Greenland, to fights between fishers and shrimp farm owners in Thailand and Ecuador. As it turned out, Spanish and Canadian fisheries bureaucrats debated the great Turbot War on the list as it was playing out on the high seas.

On AQUA-L, I began learning about the efforts shrimp farmers were making to fight a variety of viruses, in-

cluding using different chemicals and antibiotics, and changing varieties of shrimp. Salmon farmers, who raise their fish in cages, were discussing the best feeds and whether fecal matter from their caged fish were causing environmental problems.

We soon ventured out of lurk phase, and began asking questions. Some questions we posted to the list. John asked whether scientists saw a use for chaos theory in developing management plans for Atlantic fisheries. I asked for help in understanding the effects of the release of farmed salmon on wild salmon populations. We both sent out questions aimed at finding fishers or fish farmers or potential locations for our field trips. Other questions we sent to individual list participants, asking for a copy of a particular scientific paper they were discussing or for further information about a particular subject.

Oh, one other thing. The day "Oceans of Trouble" began running, I put out a note on the listservs we were using, thanking people for their help. That night and the next morning, I was literally able to watch the message move around the globe as I received responses time zone by time zone requesting copies of the series.

has gone off-point. That first message will inevitably be followed by an avalanche of E-mail responses, agreeing emphatically with the argument while apparently oblivious to the obvious irony that they are engaging in the very practice they are criticizing by writing about it in the first place! Nevertheless, the small sliver of worthwhile material is often exceptional, and worth the price of trudging through the rest of the muck. Much of the material in this book has been culled over the years from journalism-related mailing lists.

One at a Time. Subscribing to more than one mailing list at a time is a sure way of quickly getting turned off by this part of the Internet. Some mailing lists get heavy traffic, with dozens of messages each day. Signing up to multiple lists at the beginning will lead to an avalanche of E-mail.

Separate Mailing List Mail. Most E-mail programs allow users to "filter" mail into separate folders. If you have only one E-mail account, it is advisable to filter the mail from mailing lists into a folder separate from your other mail. If you have more than one account, you may want to have one just for mailing list correspondence.

Not for Daily Deadlines. Like ProfNet, mailing lists are not practical for deadline reporting. Confine the use of discussion groups to enterprise projects.

Verify Sources. As is the case with single-point E-mail contacts, you cannot be guaranteed that people on the list are who they claim to be. If you are going to pursue potential sources from a mailing list, first verify their identities.

JOURNALISM MAILING LISTS

The following lists some of the more popular journalism discussion groups available via electronic mail. Almost all of the mailing lists carry related job postings and opportunities. Following each entry below is how to subscribe to the list, a process that is explained in more detail later in the chapter (see The Mechanics of Mailing Lists). Membership numbers were from 1998.

General Journalism Topics

Reporting. IRE-L, a mailing list operated by Investigative Reporters and Editors at the University of Missouri School of Journalism, is one of the best journalism mailing lists. With about 1,300 subscribers, it is also among the most popular. Subscribers exchange and debate various reporting tips, techniques, and story ideas.

> To: listproc@lists.missouri.edu
> subscribe IRE-L (your name)

General Journalism. SPJ-L is the mailing list of the Society of Professional Journalists, the nation's oldest journalism organization. With about 1,000 members, it too is one of the largest journalism-related mailing lists. SPJ-L conversations are quite broad, ranging from the day's news and ethical dilemmas to SPJ business.

To: listserv@lists.psu.edu
subscribe SPJ-L (your name)

Computer-Assisted Reporting

Computer-assisted reporting is an obvious topic for Internet discussion groups, and there are several useful lists dealing both with data analysis and on-line searching.

CARR-L. CARR-L, which stands for Computer-Assisted Reporting and Research, is the oldest of the journalism mailing lists. It was started by Elliott Parker of Central Michigan University as "an electronic place where both working journalists and journalism educators can 'meet' and discuss 'cyberspace'." With some 1,600 subscribers, it is the largest of the non-broadcast journalism lists.

To: listserv@ulkyvm.louisville.edu
subscribe CARR-L (your name)

NICAR-L. A newer but perhaps even richer computer-assisted reporting list is NICAR-L, created by Brant Houston's team at the National Institute of Computer-Assisted Reporting, a branch of IRE at the University of Missouri. NICAR-L reported some 1,000 subscribers exchanging ideas on the various aspects of data analysis and on-line searching.

To: listproc@lists.missouri.edu
subscribe NICAR-L (your name)

NEWS LIBRARIANS. NEWSLIB was designed for news librarians and other on-line journalism researchers. Run by Barbara Semonche of the University of North Carolina School of Journalism and Mass Communication Library, much of the list's content is directly applicable for journalists trying to employ the Internet in their daily reporting. There are more than 800 members.

To: listproc@listserv.oit.unc.edu
subscribe NEWSLIB (your name)

Campaign Finance. The Campaign Finance Information Center, an arm of IRE, runs CFIC-L.

To: majordomo@campaignfinance.org
subscribe CFIC-L (your E-mail address)

INTCAR-L. INTCAR-L, the Internationally Oriented Computer-Assisted Reporting List, is a CAR mailing list for reporters around the globe. Run by American University's Chris Simpson, INTCAR-L has more than 200 subscribers.

> To: listserv@american.edu
> subscribe INTCAR-L (your name)

Beats

A growing number of electronic discussion groups center around traditional newsroom beats, affording reporters covering the same issues in different locales the opportunity to share their techniques, successes, and frustrations.

Cops and Courts. Cleveland Plain Dealer federal courts reporter Mark Rollenhagen created the Cops & Courts Reporters mailing list (CCR-L) in 1996. It has more than 200 members.

> To: majordomo@reporters.net
> subscribe CCR-L (your E-mail address)

Higher Education. The Education Writers Association operates HigherEd-L, a list for reporters who specialize in the coverage of higher education. It is a closed mailing list. Only EWA members can join. To become an association member, go to:

> www.ewa.org

Schools. EWA also runs another private mailing list, EWA-L, primarily for reporters covering kindergarten through 12th grade.

Environment. The Society of Environmental Journalists runs a private mailing list for members only to discuss environmental reporting issues. To become an SEJ member, go to:

> www.sej.org

Science. About 85 science writers subscribe to NASW-TALK, the National Association of Science Writers list.

> To: majordomo@nasw.org
> subscribe NASW-TALK

Science Freelancing. NASW also runs a science journalism list for freelance science writers.

> To: majordomo@nasw.org
> subscribe NASW-FREELANCE

Features. WriterL is unusual in that it is a fee-based mailing list. But for the $17 annual payment, plus a $5 initiation fee, members get thoughtful dialogue on feature writing, explanatory journalism, literary journalism, book journalism, and new writing techniques on this moderated list. The discussion group is led by Jon Franklin, the two-time Pulitzer Prize winner who is one of the best newspaper feature writers of his generation. To find out more about WriterL go to:

> www.bylines.org

Children and Families. Kidbeat is the mailing list of the Casey Journalism Center for Children and Families, the University of Maryland institute led by former *Wall Street Journal* correspondent Cathy Trost. It is designed for reporters specializing in coverage of children and family issues, but members also include scholars and analysts who can be sources for stories.

> To: listserv@umdd.umd.edu
> subscribe KIDBEAT (your name)

International Reporting. CORREX-L is a discussion group for foreign correspondents "to communicate working conditions, seek and impart assistance to other list-members, and generally try to make life easier for everyone on foreign assignment." It grew to more than 500 members in its first two years.

> To: majordomo@true.net
> subscribe CORREX-L (your E-mail address)

Religion. Religion writers can turn to JREL-L "to share information resources, points of view on religious issues, and article ideas." The list, operated by Tim Morgan of *Christianity Today* magazine, had nearly 200 members.

> To: majordomo@iclnet93.iclnet.org
> subscribe JRE-L (your E-mail address)

Specialties around the Newsroom

Some mailing lists, such as the following, deal with specific nonreporting newsroom jobs.

Copyediting. COPYEDITING-L is a discussion group for copy editors "and other defenders of the English language who want to discuss anything related to editing: sticky style issues; philosophy of editing; newspaper, technical, and other specialized editing; reference books; client relations; Internet resources; electronic editing and software; freelance issues, and so on." The Cornell University-based list had more than 850 members.

> To: listproc@cornell.edu
> subscribe COPYEDITING-L (your name)

Editorial Writers. NCEW-L is a closed list run by Phineas Fiske of *Newsday* for the National Conference of Editorial Writers. To join the list's 200 editorial writers, contact Fiske at:

> pfiske@netusa.net

Photographers. More than 1,000 news photographers, photo editors, graphics editors, and others belong to NPPA-L, the National Press Photographers Association discussion list.

> To: listserv@cmuvm.csv.cmich.edu
> subscribe NPPA-L (your name)

On-line Publishing

The emergence of on-line newspapers has triggered the creation of discussion groups devoted to the topic.

On-line News. Steve Outing, an on-line publishing pioneer, operates ONLINE-NEWS to discuss and exchange ideas on "the transition of traditional news media into the on-line world." An automated E-mail form to subscribe to the list is available at:

> www.planetarynews.com/online-news

On-line Newspapers. Another Outing list, ONLINE-NEWSPAPERS, is a closed discussion group for "newspaper people" only. It is more narrowly focused on electronic newspapers than the open ONLINE-NEWS list, which includes other media. Submit E-mail via:

www.planetarynews.com/online-newspapers

FOIA and Press Law

Freedom of Information. Barbara Croll Fought at Syracuse University's Newhouse School of Public Communications created FOI-L for the National Freedom of Information Coalition. The discussion group, with more than 450 members, "is designed as a place to post information, get FOI questions answered, discuss trends in the law, share it-worked-for-us stories, collaborate on getting access to public records and support the public's right to know."

To: listserv@listserv@syr.edu
subscribe FOI-L (your name)

Press Law Updates. This list provides subscribers with biweekly digest versions of the Reporters Committee for Freedom of the Press's News Media Update, which provides snapshots of the latest developments in laws and legal rulings affecting journalists. This is not a discussion group.

To: rcfp@rcfp.org
subscribe (your name)

Broadcast Regulation. COMLAW-L focuses on regulatory issues surrounding broadcasting, cable TV, and the Internet. It is run by the American Association of Law Schools section on mass communications law. Many of the 400-plus members are communication attorneys and law professors.

To: listproc@lawlib.wuacc.edu
subscribe COMLAW-L

Journalism Issues

Journalism Ethics. The Society of Professional Journalists runs SPJ-ETHICS, a separate mailing list with about 250 members. It specializes in discussions and debates on journalism ethics.

To: majordomo@dworkin.wustl.edu
subscribe SPJ-ETHICS (your E-mail address)

More Ethics. JOURNETHICS is a much smaller discussion group on journalism ethics.

> To: listproc@lists.missouri.edu
> subscribe JOURNETHICS (your name)

Diversity. In 1997, the National Association of Black Journalists (NABJ) became the first minority journalism group to create a mailing list. The NABJ list, created at the University of Maryland College of Journalism, includes discussions on newsroom diversity issues.

> To: listserv@umdd.umd.edu
> subscribe NABJ (your name)

Working Conditions. The Canadian-based Guildnet-L list focuses on "unionism, labor/management, health and safety, pay and equity, and other related issues."

> To: majordomo@acs.ryerson.ca
> subscribe Guildnet-L (your E-mail address)

Broadcast Journalism

ShopTalk. ShopTalk is a mailing list, but not a discussion group. Instead the system distributes each weekday a newsletter about TV news. Written by media consultant Don Fitzpatrick and distributed by the Syracuse University Newhouse School of Public Communications, ShopTalk is by far the most popular journalism-related mailing list, with more than 8,000 subscribers.

> listserv@listserv.syr.edu
> subscribe ShopTalk (your name)

RTVJ-L. RTVJ-L was created by the Radio–Television Journalism Division of the Association for Education in Journalism and Mass Communication as a general broadcast journalism discussion group for professionals, academics, and students. It has about 450 members.

> listproc@server.umt.edu
> subscribe RTVJ-L (your name)

BRDCST-L. The Broadcast Discussion List is similar to RTVJ-L in both size and mission.

listserv@unlvm.unl.edu
subscribe BRDCST-L (your name)

Student Journalism

Student Media. The STUMEDIA list, with more than 400 members, is for students involved in campus newspapers, TV, radio, and other news outlets.

To: listserv@uabdpo.dpo.uab.edu
subscribe STUMEDIA (your name)

Campus SPJ. SPJ-C is for campus chapters of the Society of Professional Journalists.

To: listserv@umdd.umd.edu
subscribe SPJ-C (your name)

College Media Advisers. CMA-L is for advisers to college newspapers and other media. It is a closed list. To subscribe, write to list owner Eddie Blick at:

blick@latech.edu

Student Electronic Newspapers. STUEPAP is a list for on-line campus newspapers.

To: listserv@vm.temple.edu
subscribe STUEPAP (your name)

Journalism Education

Journalism Educators. JOURNET-L is a popular (nearly 700 subscribers) discussion list for journalism educators.

To: listserv@american.edu
subscribe JOURNET-L (your name)

More Journalism Educators. JEANET is a smaller (about 100 subscribers) journalism educators' mailing list based in Australia.

To: majordomo@uow.edu.au
subscribe JEANET (your E-mail address)

Journalism History. JHISTORY is "a meeting place for journalism and mass communication historians to discuss academic and professional issues." About 300 scholars subscribe to the New York University–based list.

> To: listproc@lists.nyu.edu
> subscribe JHISTORY (your name)

FINDING MAILING LISTS

There are several searchable lists of mailing lists on the Web, although, like all other search tools on the Internet, none are comprehensive. They include:

Reference.Com. This is a powerful site with more than 100,000 mailing lists indexed, searchable by keyword. It is available at:

> www.reference.com

Remember to change the menu to "Mailing List Directory" before searching.

Liszt. Liszt had indexed 84,792 mailing lists by early 1998, searchable by keyword. It also provides a directory-style search function for larger mailing lists. Liszt can be accessed at:

> www.liszt.com

L-Soft International. L-Soft, which operates the Listserv system, has a database of the 15,944 public Listserv mailing lists. It is at:

> www.lsoft.com/lists/listref.html

THE MECHANICS OF MAILING LISTS

The Address. To use mailing lists you have to understand a bit about how they function. There are three things needed to operate a mailing list—the name of the list, the name of the computer system that is hosting the list, and the type of system that operates the list (such as Listserv, Listproc, or Majordomo). When you want to tell the computer system something—such as to sign you up, drop you from the list, or provide information about who is on the list—you need to send a command to the computer. The way to contact the computer is to send an E-mail. The portion of the E-mail address before the @ sign must be the type of system (Listserv, Listproc, Majordomo, etc.). The part after the @ symbol must be the computer host address.

When you want to send a note to the membership of the list, then the first part of the E-mail address must be the name of the list, and the second part the computer host address. This seems fairly straightforward, but it is easy to send a message intended for the list members mistakenly to the computer (which the computer will bounce back to you in a state of confusion), or conversely to send a command intended for the computer to the list members (which will invariably lead to subscribers smugly pointing out the errors of your ways). Just remember, the last part of the address is always the computer host. When you want to write to the list, send to the list name. When you want to tell the computer to do something, write to the computer system. Here is an example for the popular mailing list CARR-L (Computer-Assisted Research & Reporting). The name of the list is CARR-L, the system is Listserv, and the computer host address is

ulkyvm.louisville.edu

To send any command to the computer, type in the Send To box:

listserv@ulkyvm.louisville.edu

To send a message to fellow list members, type in the Send To box:

CARR-L@ulkyvm.louisville.edu

Subscribing. In the Send To command box, type in the name of the mailing list type (Listserv, etc.), then an @ symbol followed by the computer host address. Leave the Cc:, Subject:, and Attachment: lines blank and move to the text portion of the screen. Use the same procedure when sending any command to the computer. If you are signing up on a Listserv or Listproc system, write in the text box:

subscribe (name of list) (your full name)

For Majordomo, write:

subscribe (list name) (your E-mail address)

Signing Off. To get off a mailing list in all three systems, set up your E-mail address as detailed above, then write in the text:

unsubscribe (list name)

Sending Messages. To send a message to the list members, type in the Send box:

LIST NAME@COMPUTER HOST ADDRESS

Before crafting a message, spend a moment thinking of a subject line that is going to catch the eye of readers. This is critical. Often mail list subscribers get so many messages they may not even open up every message, let alone read each one carefully. Think of the subject lines as story slugs on a wire service. When I was at the Associated Press, writing catchy slugs was an art form because we knew wire editors would be more likely to open up and read stories that had compelling slugs. Subject lines that say "In Need Of Help" probably are not going to get much response. Craft the subject line around the topic of your question or comment.

Replying to Messages. There is nothing more embarrassing than wanting to respond to an individual on the list, but sending the message to the entire list instead. Remember, if you hit the "reply" button, the message will be sent to the entire list, not just the person who originated the message. Instead, look at the E-mail address in the "From" line at the top of the original E-mail, then write a new E-mail using that address if you want to reply to just that person and not the entire list. Furthermore, if you are posting a query for a story, you should specify that you would like respondents to write back to you directly, rather than the list.

Other Commands. There are other useful commands for each mailing list system, including temporarily stopping a list, obtaining a list of subscribers, getting a digest of messages, and getting message indexes. Once you sign up for a list, you will receive a document that details the various commands. Save this document for future use. If you have signed up for a mailing list but no longer have the command list, there are Web sites where you can turn.

For Listserv instructions, go to Listserv's operator L-Soft at:

www.lsoft.com/lists/listref.html

For Listproc instructions, go to its operator, Corporation for Research and Educational Networking, at:

www.cren.net/listproc/docs/usercard.html

BOX 10.2

Neil Reisner, a reporter at the Miami Herald, *was a pioneer in the use of mailing lists for reporting. Here, he describes how he used lists for a cover story on disabled journalists for the* American Journalism Review.

In the beginning, back before there was a World Wide Web or universal E-mail, back before Windows 95 or even Windows 3.0, back when DOS ruled and gophers were still garden pests, back, say, as far as 1990, there were cyberspace's forebears: Computerized bulletin board systems (BBSs) run by teenage hackers in their basements; informal networks like Fidonet, a network of BBSs around the country and the world that relayed messages back and forth to one another on a regular schedule, an Internet-like creation invented before mere mortals were allowed on the Internet. Those were the on-line places where some of us began experimenting with the notion that these new ways of communicating could somehow be brought to bear on journalism. We weren't seeking data to download or the latest Census report in PDF format. We were looking for sources, human beings we could interview, folks we wouldn't likely find another way.

What do I mean? Let me tell you about a story that appeared in December 1991 in the *Washington Journalism Review*, now known as *American Journalism Review*, about journalists with disabilities. I wrote it with Annemarie Cooke, a former New Jersey reporting colleague and herself legally blind.

The problem was that, other than a Garden State broadcaster who used a wheelchair, a visually impaired magazine writer, and Annemarie, who had been an ace police reporter, we didn't know a whole lot of journalists with disabilities. The challenge? Where to find some.

I'd been playing around on CompuServe and thought there might be some possibilities there. I posted two messages, one to CompuServe's Journalism Forum and another to its forum on disabilities (reached on-line with the cheerlike command, "Go Disabilities"), asking whether anyone might possibly know anyone else who fit the bill. I watched with amazement as the replies poured into my E-mailbox. We learned about Bob Fuss, a veteran correspondent who covered Capitol Hill for NBC and Mutual Radio, who used crutches and covered the Loma Prieta earthquake outside San Francisco in 1989 and Ferdinand Marcos's departure from the Philippines

We found Henry Kisor, book editor for the *Chicago Sun-Times,* who was deaf and whom I interviewed on-line—the phone really wouldn't have helped—using the BBS he'd set up at his home so friends could contact him.

We learned that ABC's John Hockenberry, then Mid-East correspondent for NPR and just returned from covering the Kurdish refugees after The Gulf War, uses a wheelchair.

We found blind television and newspaper reporters, editors who were deaf, and whole bunches of journalists with one or another congenital disability.

My point? Had we not done our reporting on-line, we likely never would have learned about them. Nothing in Bob Fuss's or John Hockenberry's

(Continued)

BOX 10.2 *Continued*

voices would ever tell us they had difficulty walking. Nothing in Henry Kisor's reviews told readers that he was deaf. Nothing in the copy filed by blind newspaper reporters told us they couldn't see.

Only by reaching out via cyberspace did we find them. I often fear that the explosive sexiness of the World Wide Web, how easy it makes finding information, and the allure of downloading huge data sets we can analyze for all measure of skullduggery obscures one of the on-line world's simplest and finest characteristics: It's a terrific place to find folks with stories, folks whose stories we can tell.

We should remember that. Because at the end of the day, that's what we're supposed to do.

For Majordomo instructions, go to the following Ohio State University site:

www.cis.ohio-state.edu/~barr/majordomo-faq.html

For commands on the Lyris system, go to:

www.lyris.com/help/LyrisEmailCommands.html

Searching Mail Archives. Some lists provide commands to retrieve archived messages from the list. One company, Find Mail, has created a database that allows a user to search thousands of mailing list archives at the same time. It is located at:

www.findmail.com

LOVE ON THE LISTSERV: A FISH STORY

Many journalists have wonderful success stories to tell in using mailing lists in their reporting, but none comes close to that told by John McQuaid. The New Orleans *Times-Picayune* reporter signed on to Fishfolk, a Listserv on fisheries issues, in the course of researching the paper's series on oceans. "Oceans of Trouble" went on to win the 1997 Pulitzer prize for Public Service, and McQuaid and partner Mark Schleifstein's use of mailing lists played an integral role (see p. 87). But winning the Pulitzer was "just icing on the cake," McQuaid said. That's because another regular Fishfolk contributor was Trish Clay, an anthropologist at the National Marine Fisheries Service in Woods Hole, Massachusetts. When she posted a message on Fishfolk saying she was taking a temporary assignment at the State Department in Washington, where McQuaid was assigned, he E-mailed her requesting an interview. "We met for lunch and the rest is, as they say, history." Today they are married and living in Louisiana.

▶ 11

Newsgroups: Electronic Bulletin Boards

Newsgroups are similar to mailing groups: They provide a place where people on the Internet with similar interests gather and discuss specific issues. And like the mailing groups discussed in the previous chapter, newsgroups can be useful to journalists "listening in" to special-interest groups, seeking out sources, or asking questions of a particular group.

But mailing lists and newsgroups operate differently. The difference between mailing lists and newsgroups is like the difference between a magazine subscription and a bulletin board. Mailing lists, like magazine subscriptions, automatically provide you with all of the information being circulated as soon as you subscribe. Newsgroups are more like bulletin boards in that the reader has to actively go to a particular place in order to read the materials.

More than 250,000 "articles" are posted around the globe each day on the Usenet system, according to Reference.Com, an Internet search tool for newsgroups and mailing lists. There are more than 50,000 newsgroups, according to Deja News, another search product for newsgroups.

JOURNALISTIC USES

Journalists can use newsgroups for the same reasons as mailing lists: Finding sources and "listening in" on a particular issue. But while mailing lists are best for contacting expert sources, newsgroups excel in finding "real people."

Putting a Face on the Story. Mike Antonucci of the *San Jose Mercury News* calls it "sometimes the most elusive quarry in any assignment, a cross section of average human beings who illustrate why you're doing the story in the first place." Antonucci has used newsgroups to find local people to illustrate the growing interest in genealogy and battles over satellite dish installations. Of course, reporters tapping into newsgroups for sources need to verify the identity of the people found, as discussed in the mailing list chapter. Also, remember that people who use Internet newsgroups do not represent a cross section of society. They are generally more affluent and educated (just by virtue of the fact that they have access to a computer) than the general population.

BOX 11.1

Steven Eisenstadt was the Raleigh News & Observer's *high technology reporter when he employed the Web, newsgroups, and E-mail to track down a late-breaking story on layoffs at a local company.*

The phone rang at 4 P.M. the Friday before Labor Day weekend. A tipster wanted to tell the *News & Observer* business section that a local software company had handed out a large number of pink slips earlier in the day. The tipster was not directly involved, though, and knew few details.

I immediately called the company and got only voice mailboxes. Because the company wasn't particularly large or well known, I had no contacts there. But I needed some, and fast.

Enter the Internet.

Whenever someone posts to an Internet newsgroup, whether to sell a sofa or debate the best Who album, the poster's E-mail address (and sometimes his or her name) is included. I figured that if the company had its own Internet domain name, I could obtain the E-mail addresses of any employee who had ever posted to a newsgroup

from work. I fired up Netscape and went to Deja News. A search of "imonics.com" produced more than a dozen hits. One Imonics employee had posted a comment to a technical computer newsgroup a few months earlier; another was trying to sell a used CD player. Some of the postings had "sigs" at the bottom containing the poster's names! I simply got the phone book and looked up the employees' home numbers. On my first call, I reached a guy who not only was one of the downsizees but told me how some employees who knew the layoffs were coming mocked the situation by coming to their last day of work dressed as Dilbert.

By the time the company vice president called me back around 5 P.M., I had the whole story and only needed him to confirm the information, which he did.

Finding Specific People. Sometimes newsgroups are the best way to track down a specific "real person" involved in a story. For example, the *Philadelphia Inquirer* used a newsgroup posting to find a group of local University of Delaware students who were in Japan during a major earthquake. Steven Eisenstadt tracked down employees of a local company facing layoffs for the *Raleigh News & Observer* (see p. 104).

Listening In. Lurking around on newsgroups connected to an issue beat or a geographical area can generate story ideas through discussions about a new issue or emerging concern. Reporters should search for newsgroups on their specific issues and local city.

Expert Sources. Newsgroups can be used to locate experts in much the same way as mailing lists, but the mailing groups, which have more professionally oriented groups, usually produce better results.

HOW NEWSGROUPS WORK

Usenet is accessed through special newsreader software. This software already is built in to both Netscape and Explorer. To access through Netscape, click on the Windows menu and select Netscape News. In Explorer, go to the Mail button and select Read News. From there you can read and post messages.

NEWSGROUP STRUCTURE

Newsgroups are structured by large categories, or hierarchies, such as science, recreation, or computers. Those categories are then broken down by topic and sub-topic, divided by dots. For instance,

sci.environment.waste

There are seven major Usenet hierarchies:

Comp. Computer and computer science.

News. Usenet and Internet issues.

Rec. Hobbies and recreational activities.

Sci. Sciences.

Soc. Social issues and socializing.

Talk. Debate of controversial topics.

Misc. A wide variety of miscellaneous topics that do not clearly fall into one of the other major hierarchies.

There are dozens of other hierarchies. The most popular is "alt," which covers "alternative" topics.

FINDING NEWSGROUPS

There are Usenet search engines available on the Web to help locate specific newsgroups. Of course, as with the engines to search Web sites, none are comprehensive. Here are some of the more popular newsgroup search tools and their Web addresses:

> Reference.Com.   www.reference.com
> Liszt   www.liszt.com/news
> Tile.Net   tile.net/news
> Cyberfiber   www.cyberfiber.com

A quick search on the word *journalism* shows the power—and limitations—of newsgroup search tools. Reference.Com came back with the most hits, 21, with newsgroups covering everything from photo journalism and student journalism to alt.journalism.gonzo, devoted to the journalistic style made famous by Hunter S. Thompson. But the search did not reveal three other journalism-related discussion groups found by other search engines. Liszt found 17 journalism matches, failing to discover five others. Tile.Net uncovered 15 but failed on seven others, while Cyberfind found 13 and missed 10.

Liszt, Tile.Net, and Cyberfiber also have directory-based search options.

SEARCHING NEWSGROUPS

Several Internet search tools enable users to search thousands of newsgroups simultaneously. Deja News is the most popular, although some of the major search engines, such as Infoseek and AltaVista, now provide newsgroup search functions. In Deja News, located at:

> www.dejanews.com

users can use keywords to search more than two years' worth of archives on more than 50,000 discussion groups. Searches can be conducted by topics, author, or E-mail address. Deja News is one of the most popular Internet tools for journalists.

Professional Development

There is life after J-school. Over the last 20 years, the journalism profession has seen an explosive growth of journalism organizations, institutes, and programs designed to help working journalists improve their craft through continuing education programs, workshops and conferences, reporting and writing tools and techniques, fellowships, awards, research on a wide variety of press topics, and job listings.

THE BEST JOURNALISM WEB SITES

The information available on the Internet about journalism is so rich it is hard to highlight the best, but I have found the following Web sites to be the most useful for the widest variety of journalists and student journalists.

The Freedom Forum. Consider making the *Free!*, the Freedom Forum on-line publication (see Figure 12.1), your home page. It's that good. Adam Clayton Powell III and Co. have put together a dynamic publication that provides readers with the top breaking stories about journalism, the First Amendment, and technology in addition to Freedom Forum studies, conferences, and programs.

www.freedomforum.org

American Journalism Review. *AJR*'s NewsLink provides one of the best hyperlinked compilations of newspapers worldwide (p. 52), listings of dozens of awards and fellowships available to journalists, an archived

FIGURE 12.1   The Freedom Forum's *Free!* is both eye-catching and substantive.

Courtesy of "free" the online service of The Freedom Forum.

index of *AJR* stories, full texts of selected *AJR* articles, and original columns on on-line journalism.

www.ajr.org

Society of Professional Journalists (SPJ). The *Electronic Journalist*, the online publication of SPJ, includes daily news stories on press issues and a list of more than 60 journalism contests in addition to information on SPJ awards, reports, and conventions.

www.spj.org

Investigative Reporters and Editors (IRE). IRE's Web site (see Figure 12.2) includes a searchable database of more than 11,000 investigative reporting story abstracts, handouts developed by speakers at IRE conferences, campaign finance data and sources, and a directory of investigative reporters worldwide, plus details on IRE contests, programs, and conferences.

www.ire.org

FIGURE 12.2 *Investigative Reporters and Editors* **is rich in tips and techniques for reporters.**

Courtesy of Investigative Reporters and Editors, Inc.

The Poynter Institute for Media Studies. Poynter's weeklong workshops are some of the best journalism educational opportunities available. Poynter On-line provides details on the seminars and includes presentations and research from the institute on topics from newspaper management to newsroom diversity.

www.poynter.org

Reporters Committee for Freedom of the Press. The committee provides some of the most practical tools for reporters, such as the Freedom of Information Act letter generator (p. 31), state laws on open records and public meetings (p. 31), updates on Freedom of Information cases from around the country, and a legal defense hotline for journalists.

www.rcfp.org

NEWSROOM SPECIALISTS

Computer-Assisted Reporters. The National Institute for Computer-Assisted Reporting, operated by IRE and the University of Missouri School of Journalism, provides listings of the government databases that can be purchased through NICAR for data analysis projects. There also is information on NICAR conferences, training programs, and consulting services.

www.nicar.org

Editorial Writers. The National Conference of Editorial Writers Web site features editorial exchanges and critiques, links to on-line resources for editorial page writers, and NCEW events and programs.

www.ncew.org

Copy Editors. One of the newest journalism associations, the American Copy Editors Society, has a Web site that includes discussion boards, survey data on life as a copy editor, editing advice, copyediting references, and job opportunities.

www.copydesk.org

News Designers. The Society of News Designers is devoted to the design of newspapers, magazines, and news-oriented Web sites. The site includes a job bank, society information, and other resources for news designers, graphic artists, photographers, and students.

web.snd.org

Photographers. National Press Photographers Association On-line provides information on NPPA programs, contests, and activities. Its front page features recent award-winning news photos.

sunsite.unc.edu/nppa

International Journalists. The International Center for Journalists (formerly the Center for Foreign Journalists) outlines exchange and fellowship programs for U.S. journalists to work abroad and foreign journalists to work in the United States, a database and newsletter on central and eastern European press issues, and information on the center's workshops, seminars, and conferences.

www.icfj.org

Freelance Writers. The National Writers Union, a labor union for freelance writers, has a Web site designed to assist freelancers with information on rights and risks of freelancing and contract advice.

www.igc.org/nwu

More Freelancers. The American Society of Journalists and Authors is for freelance journalists and authors.

www.asja.org

Ombudsmen. The Organization of News Ombudsmen can be contacted at:

www5.infi.net/ono

BEATS

Education. The Education Writers Association provides a site for reporters on the schools and higher education beats, including Web resources and contest information.

www.ewa.org

Business. The Society of American Business Editors and Writers (SABW) features the Best in the Business contest, Web links for business reporters, a resumé bank, and SABW conference and program information.

www.sabew.org

Environment. The Society of Environmental Journalists (SEJ) provides linked Web resources, job opportunities, and SEJ membership and conference information.

www.sej.org

Science. One of the oldest journalism organizations, the National Association of Science Writers features guides and advice for science writers and convention updates.

www.nasw.org

Children and Families. The Casey Journalism Center for Children and Families offers resources and articles about coverage of disadvantaged children and their families.

casey.umd.edu

Washington Correspondents. The Regional Reporters Association represents Washington correspondents who cover the nation's capital from a local perspective.

www.rra.org

Specializations. The Knight Center for Specialized Journalism offers one- and two-week seminars on a wide variety of journalism specialties.

www.inform.umd.edu/knight

JOURNALISM MAGAZINES

American Journalism Review, the monthly press critique published by the University of Maryland College of Journalism (see Figure 12.3).

www.ajr.org

Columbia Journalism Review, the monthly press review published by Columbia University Graduate School of Journalism.

www.cjr.org

Editor & Publisher Interactive, the on-line version of the weekly magazine.

www.mediainfo.com

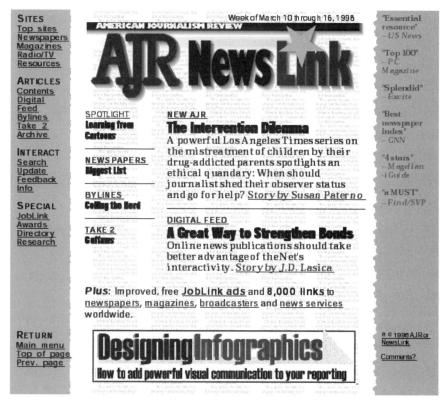

FIGURE 12.3   American Journalism Review's *NewsLink* is one of the most popular journalism sites on the Internet.

Used by permission.

The American Editor, the monthly magazine of the American Society of Newspaper Editors.

www.asne.org/kiosk/editor/tae.htm

Presstime, the monthly magazine of the Newspaper Association of America.

www.naa.org/presstime/index.html

Nieman Reports, the journal of the Nieman Foundation at Harvard University.

www.Nieman.harvard.edu/nreports.html

Online Journalism Review, an on-line publication from the Annenberg School of Communication at the University of Southern California that critiques on-line news.

www.ojr.org

MINORITY JOURNALISM ORGANIZATIONS

These organizations provide information on newsroom diversity issues and group events, programs, and convention information.

National Association of Black Journalists

www.nabj.org

National Association of Hispanic Journalists

www.nahj.org

Asian American Journalism Association

www.aaja.org

National Lesbian & Gay Journalists Association

www.nlgja.org

National Association of Minority Media Executives

www.namme.org

NEWSPAPER MANAGEMENT & LEADERSHIP

American Society of Newspaper Editors

www.asne.org

Associated Press Managing Editors

www.apme.com

American Press Institute

www.newspaper.org

Newspaper Association of America

www.naa.org

National Newspaper Association

www.oweb.com/naa/home.html

JOURNALISM RESEARCH

Freedom Forum Media Studies Center

www.freedomforum.org/whoweare/media.asp

Pew Research Center for the People and the Press

www.people-press.org

Joan Shorenstein Center for Press, Politics and Public Policy

www.ksg.harvard.edu/~presspol/home.htm

Annenberg Washington Program in Communications Policy Studies

www.annenberg.nwu.edu

Freedom Forum First Amendment Center

www.arin.k12.pa.us/~armstrong/1stamend/forum.html

Committee to Protect Journalists

www.cpj.org

Project for Excellence in Journalism

www.journalism.org

Committee of Concerned Journalists

www.journalism.org/AnnArborag.htm

John S. and James L. Knight Foundation

www.knightfdn.org

Association for Education in Journalism and Mass Communication

www.aejmc.sc.edu

THE FUTURE OF JOURNALISM

Planetary News. An electronic publication devoted to the emerging world of on-line newspapers.

www.planetarynews.com

Pew Center for Civic Journalism. The center funds experiments in civic journalism

www.pewcenter.org

New Directions for News. An institute that fosters innovation in newspapers

www.missouri.edu/~ndnwww.about.html

WOMEN IN JOURNALISM

Journalism and Women Symposium

www.jaws.org

National Federation of Press Women

www.lcc.whecn.edu/scc/cheyenne/nfpw/index.html

Association for Women in Communications

www.womcom.org

BROADCAST JOURNALISM

Radio Television News Directors Association

ww.rtnda.org

National Association of Broadcasters

www.nab.org

Broadcast Pioneers Library of American Broadcasting

www.lib.umd.edu/UMCP/LAB

OTHER JOURNALISM GROUPS

Newseum. The Freedom Forum's museum dedicated to journalism and journalists

www.newseum.org

National Press Club. The Web site provides information about the various National Press Club events, awards, scholarships, and services.

npc.press.org

Freedom of Information Coalition. This group is a coalition of various state First Amendment and open government organizations.

www.reporters.net/nfoic

The Reporters Network. Founded by *Houston Chronicle* reporter Bob Sablatura to "promote the Internet as a research and communications medium for working journalists," the network provides free E-mail and a directory of journalists.

www.reporters.net

The Newspaper Guild. The home page of the newspaper union includes highlights from the current issue of the *Guild Reporter.*

www3.newsguild.org/tng

COLLEGE JOURNALISM

Student Press Law Center. The Web site provides the full text of the *SPLC Report* magazine, news and information on laws and rulings that affect the student press, an on-line legal clinic, and a fill-in-the-blanks form for public records requests for each state.

www.splc.org

Internships and Job Opportunities. The University of Maryland's Greig Stewart has put together a hyperlinked list of various internship and job opportunity lists.

www.inform.umd.edu/EdRes/Colleges/JOUR/intern/
jobbank.html

Dow Jones Newspaper Fund. These pages detail the fund's various college and high school journalism programs, internships, and scholarships.

www.dowjones.com/newsfund

College Media Advisers. The site outlines CMA conventions and activities.

www.collegemedia.org

HIGH SCHOOL JOURNALISM

Journalism Education Association

www.spub.ksu.edu/~jea

Columbia Scholastic Press Association

www.columbia.edu/cu/cspa

National Scholastic Press Association

studentpress.journ.umn.edu

Quill & Scroll

www.uiowa.edu/~quill-sc

JOURNALISM HOBBIES

The Classic Typewriter Page

xavier.xu.edu:8000/~polt/typewriters.html

Newspaper Collectors Society of America

www.historybuff.com

► 13

The Future of the Internet as a Reporting Tool

Rule No. 1 in talking about the Internet is—or at least should be—never make predictions. The Net in the late 1990s was still a dynamic, constantly evolving entity, and suffered from the growing pains of rapid expansion. But an examination of the recent past can help us identify trends that may affect the future of reporting that uses the Internet. Those trends—from the reporter's perspective—are decidedly mixed.

CONTENT

In the first five years of the World Wide Web, the quality of its content—from a journalistic perspective—grew as quickly as its enormous growth in quantity. And without question, the richest area for reporters has been in the government Web sites containing documents and data. That growth hopefully will continue.

The commercial side of the Web also has grown in quality, but the trend there has been toward more fee-based sites where companies give the user a taste of the material available, then require flat subscription or per-use fees. Whether that will continue will depend on the ability of commercial Web sites to make more money from fee-based sites or from selling advertising space on largely free sites.

PRIVACY

Privacy concerns endanger the content quality of the Internet for reporters. On the commercial side, most Web telephone directories already have pulled their crisscross directory functions off the Net, and developments on the government side are even more disturbing. A 1997 federal law bars journalists access to drivers' records, which have been a basic newsroom tool for everything from checking school bus drivers' personal driving performance to checking the attendees of Ku Klux Klan meetings. The law came from politicians' knee-jerk reaction to the murder of TV sit-com actress Rebecca Schaeffer at her Los Angeles home by an obsessed fan. The stalker found her home address through her driving records. The irony here is that the convicted murderer hired a private investigator to get the driving record, and PIs are one of the many special-interest groups that Congress exempted from the law. Nevertheless, the law was roundly applauded and supported by both sides of the political spectrum, and triggered consideration of future shutdowns of other vital public records that happen to contain personal data, such as voting registration rolls. While driving records never were on the Internet (the law was passed in 1994 when the Web was still in its infancy), the precedent and shrill tone from politicians on privacy issues should be cause for more than a little concern in newsrooms around the country.

ACCESS

Massive delays to access the Internet through large providers such as America Online have made headlines, but that is a somewhat predictable outgrowth of the surging popularity of the Internet in the mid- and late-1990s. Despite the problems, once users got on-line, they found access to the Internet faster as modem speeds increased and other options, such as connections through phone companies, became available. And the cost went in only one direction—down. The pay-by-the-hour fee structure was replaced swiftly by flat fees, and those, too, dropped dramatically in a few short years. Also during this period, more newsrooms worked to get reporters and editors desktop access to the Internet.

NEWSROOM INTRANETS

The late 1990s saw a growth in newsroom intranets, internal Web sites that enable reporters in the newsroom or in far-flung bureaus to access a wide variety of databases easily. The Associated Press pioneered newsroom intranets, and this area has the potential for huge growth in the future.

READERSHIP CONNECTION

Small strides were made in journalists' connection to their readers as publications slowly began carrying the electronic mail addresses of reporters and editors. As more people get on-line, and more publications make their staff's E-mail addresses available, the possibilities for reporters and editors to enhance their connections to their readers and communities grow.

JOURNALISTS AS NET BELIEVERS

We are a skeptical lot by nature, so it is not surprising that journalists did not lead the charge to get on-line and incorporate the Internet into their daily reporting work. But that, too, has changed, as reporters and editors are seeing the journalistic potential of the Internet. While only a relatively small handful have all of the skills and techniques we have discussed in this book, the desire to learn is very much apparent. When Neill Borowski, director of computer-assisted reporting and analysis for the *Philadelphia Inquirer,* held his first Internet training session in the *Inquirer* newsroom, there was limited interest. "It was a curiosity," he said. A few years later in December 1997, he announced another newsroom training session. "I figured we'd need about two classes of 14 each to start with. Within two days, about 125 staff members signed up for the 28 class spots I had booked," Borowski wrote. "I've had veteran reporters pull me aside in the newsroom. With desperate looks in their eyes, they say in a whisper that they 'absolutely have to get in on the Internet training'."

CONCLUSION

The future? Well, let's not break Rule No. 1 about Internet predictions. "Who would have thought it would be what it is today?" asked Borowski. "And one can't even guess about what it will offer in the future."

I will offer not a prediction, but a hope: that the Internet becomes for all journalists what it is already for a few like Kathy Rizzo, a Washington correspondent for the Associated Press, who said: "I use the Net so much it [has] become a tool I rarely even think about."

A Journalist's Guide to the Internet: The Web Site

This book contains hundreds of Internet addresses that can help journalists do their jobs better and faster. Unfortunately, Web addresses change frequently. To take into account the ever-changing nature of the Internet, the author has created a Web version of many of the links cited in this book (see Figure A). It is available at:

reporter.umd.edu

The site is broken down by various reporting topics, such as Politics, Courts and the Law, and Records and FOIA. Links to the Web sites will be updated regularly. In addition, there is a "What's New" feature that will highlight new reporting tools that have been created since the book's publication.

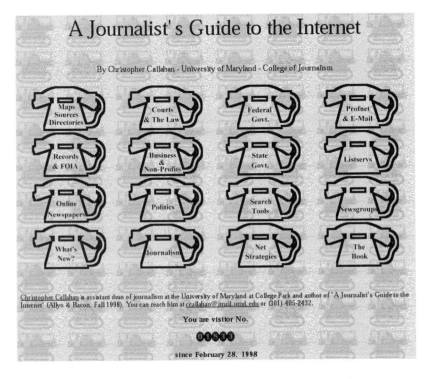

FIGURE A   The Web version of *A Journalist's Guide to the Internet* will be updated regularly.

Index